Have you wanted to get in on the knitting craze? Or do you know a little about knitting but desire to know more?

If so, this is the book for you. With our easy step-by-step picture method, you can learn all the basics of knitting in just a few hours. Putting the yarn onto the needle, or casting on, is the first step. Then there are just two stitches: the knit stitch and the purl stitch. That's all there is to it! Everything else is just a variation on these two stitches.

As you follow our learn-by-yourself lessons, you'll feel like your knitting guru is right there beside you. We've included special hints and helps to keep you moving toward the road to knitting bliss.

Once you feel comfortable with the basic techniques, you're ready to start one of our easy projects. We've included enough ideas to keeping you knitting for years.

There are a wonderful array of wearables, home decor projects and gifts for babies. We've written all of these patterns especially for the beginner.

We know this book will help you enter into the enjoyable world of knitting—a world that so many are turning to for stress relief, the camaraderie of others, an excuse to buy some colorful yarn or the simple joy of creating something wonderful.

Happy Knitting!

Note to Left Handers: *Knitting is a two-handed process in which both hands are used almost equally. We urge left handers to learn the right-handed way. It may seem awkward at first, but this is true for all beginning knitters. If the right-handed method is not learned, pattern instructions will always have to be reversed in the future—a difficult and confusing task.*

Contents

Learn to Knit Lessons:

Projects:

Supplies Needed for Practice Lessons:

- One 3½ oz skein of knitting worsted weight yarn in a light color
- Size 8 (5mm) 10-inch long straight knitting needles
- Size H/8/5mm crochet hook (for repairs)
- Scissors
- Tape measure
- Size 16 tapestry needle or plastic yarn needle

To knit, you need only a pair of knitting needles, some yarn, a pair of scissors, a tape measure and a tapestry or yarn needle. Later on, for working some of the projects in this book you can add all kinds of accessories, such as markers, stitch holders and needle point protectors. But for now, your yarn and needles are all you really need.

Yarn

Yarn comes in a wonderful selection of materials, textures, sizes and colors, ranging from wool to metallic, lumpy to smooth, gossamer fine to chunky, and from the palest pastels to vibrant neon shades.

The most commonly used yarn, and the one you'll need for the lessons in this book, is worsted weight (sometimes called 4-ply). It is readily available in a wide variety of beautiful colors. Choose a light color for practice—it will be much easier to see the individual stitches.

Always read yarn labels carefully. The label will tell you how much yarn is in the skein or ball, in ounces, grams or yards; the type of yarn; how to care for it; and sometimes how to pull the yarn from the skein (and yes, there is a trick to this!) The label usually bears a dye lot number, which assures you that the color of each skein with this same number is identical. The same color may vary from dye lot to dye lot, creating unsightly variations in color when a project is finished. So when purchasing yarn for a project, be sure to match the dye lot number on the skeins and purchase enough to complete the project.

You'll need a blunt-pointed sewing needle with an eye big enough to carry the yarn for weaving in ends and joining pieces. You can use a size 16 steel tapestry needle or purchase a large plastic sewing needle called a yarn needle.

Crochet Hooks

Even though you're knitting, not crocheting, you'll need to have a crochet hook handy for correcting mistakes, retrieving dropped stitches and for some finishing techniques. You don't need to know how to crochet, though!

The hook size you need depends on the thickness of the yarn you are using for your project and the size of the knitting needles.

Here's a handy chart to show you what size hook to use:

Knitting Needle Size	Crochet Hook Size
5, 6	F
7, 8, 9	G
10 and 10½	H
11 and 13	I
15 and 17	J

Knitting Needles

Knitting needles come in pairs of straight needles with a shaped point at one end and a knob at the other end of each needle so that the stitches won't slide off. Needles also come in sets of four double-pointed needles used for making small seamless projects, and in circular form with a point at each end.

You will most often use straight needles, which are readily available in many materials including aluminum, bamboo and plastic. The straight needles come in a variety of lengths, the most common being l0 inches and l4 inches. For our lessons, we will use the l0-inch length.

The needles also come in a variety of sizes, which refer to the diameter and thus the size of the stitch you can make with them. These are numbered from 0 (the smallest usually available) to 17 (the largest usually available). There are larger needles, but they are not used as often. For our lessons, we use a size 8 needle, an average size for use with worsted weight yarn.

Let's look at a knitting needle:

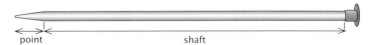

point   shaft

Now with your yarn and needles ready, let's get started.

Casting On

Knitting always starts with a row of foundation stitches worked onto one needle. Making a foundation row is called casting on. Although there are several ways of casting on, the one which follows is easiest for beginners.

Step 1:

Make a slip knot on one needle as follows: Make a yarn loop, leaving about 4 inch length of yarn at free end.

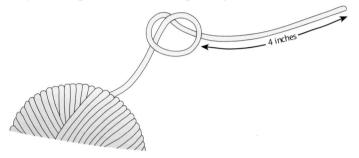

Insert knitting needle into loop and draw up yarn from free end to make a loop on needle.

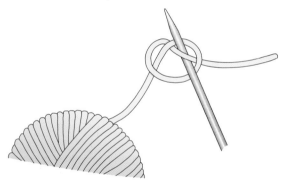

Pull yarn firmly, but not tightly, to form a slip knot on the shaft, not the point, of the needle. Pull yarn end to tighten the loop. This slip knot counts as your first stitch.

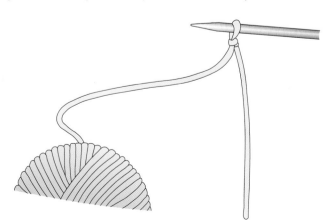

Step 2:

Place the needle with the knot in your left hand, placing the thumb and index finger close to the point of the needle, which helps you control it.

Step 3:

Hold the other needle with your right hand, again with your fingers close to the point. Grasp the needle firmly, but not tightly.

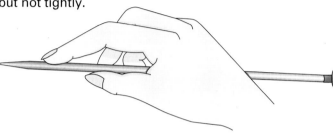

Step 4:

Your right hand controls the yarn coming from the ball. To help keep your tension even, hold the yarn loosely against the palm of your hand with three fingers, and then up and over your index finger. These diagrams show how this looks from above the hand and beneath the hand.

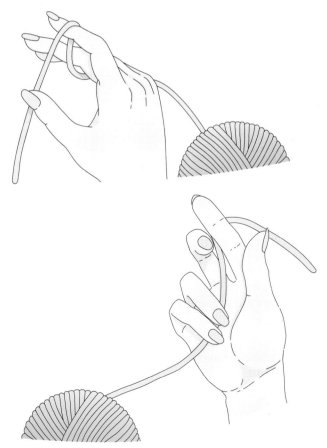

Step 5:

Insert the point of the right needle—from front to back—into the slip knot and under the left needle.

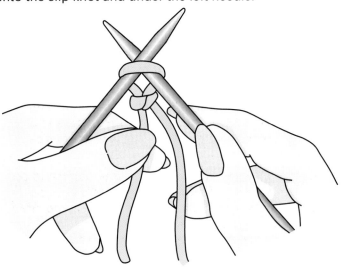

and, releasing right hand's grip on the right needle, bring yarn under and over the point of right needle.

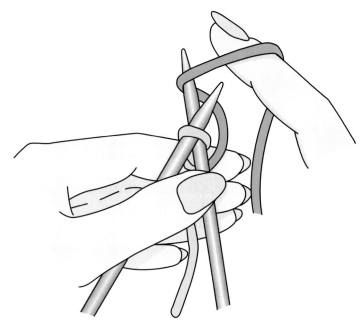

Step 6:

Continuing to hold left needle in your left hand, move left fingers over to brace right needle.

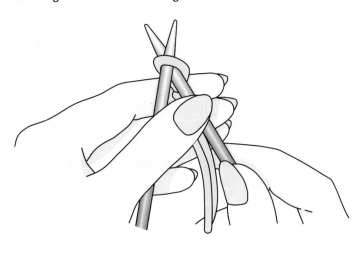

Step 7:

Returning right fingers to right needle, draw yarn through stitch with right needle.

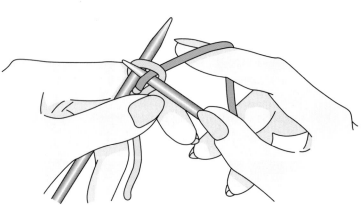

With right index finger, pick up the yarn from the ball

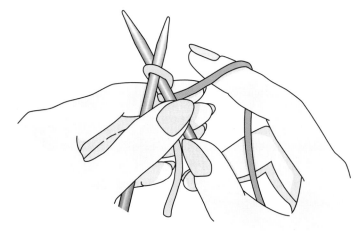

Step 8:

Slide left needle point into new stitch, then remove right needle.

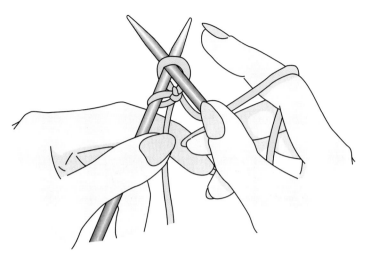

Step 9:

Pull ball of yarn gently, but not tightly, to make stitch snug on needle; you should be able to slip the stitch back and forth on the shaft of the needle easily.

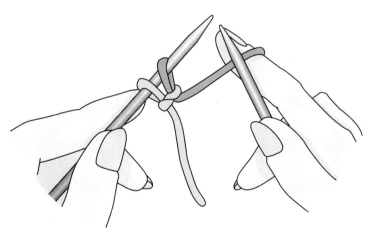

You have now made one stitch, and there are two stitches on left needle (remember the slip knot counts as a stitch).

Step 10:

Insert point of right needle—from front to back—into stitch you've just made and under left needle.

Repeat Steps 6 through 10 for next stitch.

Continue repeating Steps 6 through 10 until you have 24 stitches on the left needle. Be sure to pull each stitch up, off the point and onto the shaft of the left needle.

Now stop, relax, get a cup of coffee or a soda, and look at your work. It's probably loose or tight and uneven, which is normal for a beginner. As you practice and begin to feel less clumsy, your work will automatically become more even.

Now after all that work, guess what you're going to do next—destroy it! To do this, pull the needle out from the stitches, then wind the used yarn back on the skein or ball. Begin again and cast on 24 stitches, trying this time to work more evenly, keeping each stitch snug but not tight.

Hint: *Beginners usually knit very tightly, making it hard to slide the stitches on the needle. Try to relax; it is better to work too loosely in the beginning, than too tightly. Take care not to make your stitches on the point of the needle; instead, slide the needle shaft well through each stitch as you work. Always be sure to insert needle under full thickness of yarn, to avoid "splitting" the yarn.*

The Knit Stitch

All knitting is made up of only two basic stitches, the knit stitch and the purl stitch. These are combined in many ways to create different effects and textures. And guess what! Now you're halfway to being a knitter, for you've already learned the knit stitch as you practiced casting on! That's because the first three steps of the knit stitch are exactly like casting on.

Step 1:

Hold the needle with the 24 cast-on stitches from Lesson 1 in your left hand. Insert the point of the right needle in the first stitch, from front to back, just as in casting on.

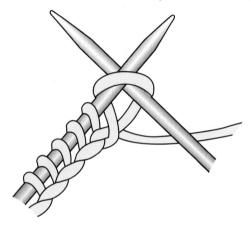

Step 2:

With right index finger, bring yarn from the skein under and over the point of the right needle.

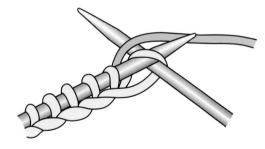

Step 3:

Draw yarn through the stitch with the right needle point.

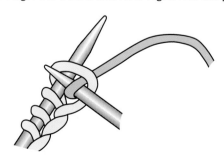

Step 4:

The next step now differs from casting on. Slip the loop on the left needle off, so the new stitch is entirely on the right needle.

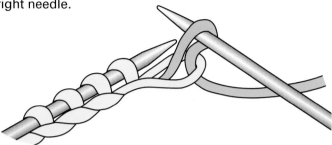

Now you've completed your first knit stitch! Repeat these four steps in each stitch remaining on the left needle. When all stitches are on the right needle and the left needle is free, another row has been completed. Turn the right needle and place it in your left hand. Hold the free needle in your right hand. Work another row of stitches in same manner as last row, taking care not to work tightly. Work 10 more rows of knit stitches.

The pattern formed by knitting every row is called *garter stitch* (we don't really know why!), and looks the same on both sides. When counting rows in garter stitch, each raised ridge indicates you have knitted two rows.

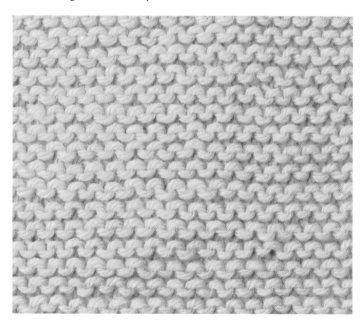

Hint: *When working on a garter stitch project it is helpful to place a small safety pin on the right side of the piece as after a few rows both sides look the same.*

Break time!

The Kaleidoscope Throw on page 34 and the Perfectly Pink Scarf on page 27 are made using only the knit stitch. If you are anxious to test your knitting skills, one of these projects is a good place to start.

The Purl Stitch

The reverse of the knit stitch is called the purl stitch. Instead of inserting the right needle point from front to back under the left needle (as you did for the knit stitch), you will now insert it from back to front, in front of the left needle. Work as follows on the 24 stitches already on your needle.

Step 1:

Insert the right needle, from right to left, into the first stitch, and in front of the left needle.

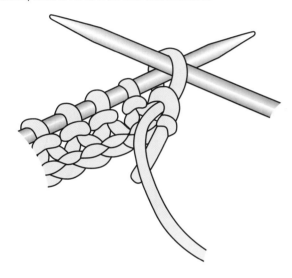

Step 2:

Holding the yarn in front of the work (side toward you), bring it around the right needle counterclockwise.

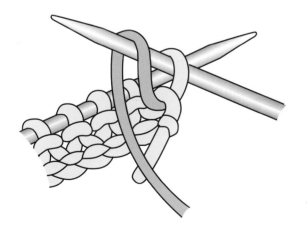

Step 3:

With the right needle, pull the yarn back through the stitch.

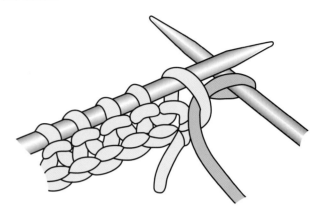

Slide the stitch off the left needle, leaving the new stitch on the right needle.

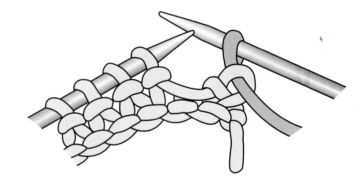

Your first purl stitch is now completed. Continue to repeat these three steps in every stitch across the row. The row you have just purled will be considered the wrong side of your work for the moment.

Now transfer the needle with the stitches from your right to left hand; the side of the work now facing you is called the right side of your work. Knit every stitch in the row; at end of row, transfer the needle with the stitches to your left hand, then purl every stitch in the row. Knit across another row, purl across another row.

Now stop and look at your work; by alternating knit and purl rows, you are creating one of the most frequently used stitch patterns in knitting, *stockinette stitch*.

Turn the work over to the right side; it should look like stitches in Photo A. The wrong side of the work should look like stitches in Photo B.

Photo B

Photo A

Continue with your practice piece, alternately knitting and purling rows, until you feel comfortable with the needles and yarn. As you work you'll see that your piece will begin to look more even.

Hint: *Hold your work and hands in a comfortable relaxed position. The more comfortable you are, the more even your work will be.*

Correcting Mistakes

Dropped Stitches

Each time you knit or purl a stitch, take care to pull the stitch off the left needle after completing the new stitch. Otherwise, you will be adding stitches when you don't want to. But if you let a stitch slip off the needle before you've knitted or purled it, it's called a dropped stitch. Even expert knitters drop a stitch now and then, but a dropped stitch must be picked up and put back on the needle. If not, the stitch will "run" down the length of the piece, just like a run in a stocking!

If you notice the dropped stitch right away, and it has not run down more than one row, you can usually place it back on the needle easily.

But if it has dropped several rows, you'll find it easier to use a crochet hook to work the stitch back up to the needle.

On the knit side (right side of work) of the stockinette stitch, insert the crochet hook into the dropped stitch from front to back, under the horizontal strand in the row above.

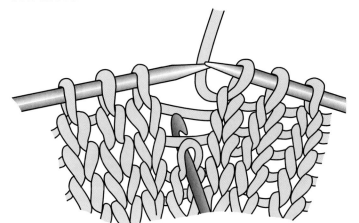

Hook the horizontal strand above and pull through the loop on the crochet hook. Continue in this manner until you reach the last row worked, then transfer the loop from the crochet hook to the left needle, being careful not to twist it.

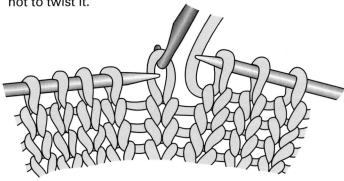

Unraveling Stitches

Sometimes it is necessary to unravel a large number of stitches, even down several rows, to correct a mistake. Whenever possible, carefully unravel the stitches one by one by putting the needle into the row below and undoing the stitch above, until the mistake is reached.

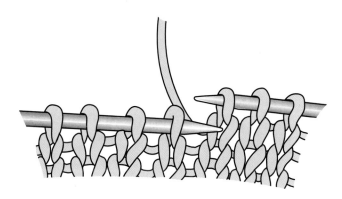

If several rows need to be unraveled, carefully slide all stitches off the needle and unravel each row down to the row in which the error occurred. Then unravel this row, stitch by stitch, placing each stitch back on the needle in the correct position, without twisting it.

Binding off

Now you've learned how to cast on, and to knit and purl the stitches; next, you need to know how to take the stitches off the needle once you've finished a piece.

The process used to secure the stitches is called binding off. Let's bind off your practice piece; be careful to work loosely for this procedure, and begin with the right side (the knit side) of your work facing you.

Knit Bind-Off

Step 1:

Knit the first 2 stitches. Now insert the left needle into the first of the 2 stitches, the one you knitted first,

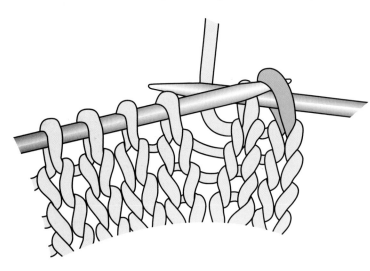

and pull it over the second stitch and completely off the needle. You have now bound off one stitch.

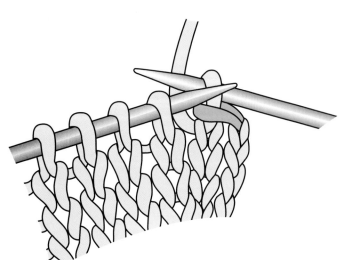

Step 2:

Knit one more stitch; insert the left needle into the first stitch on the right needle and pull the first stitch over the new stitch and completely off the needle. Another stitch is now bound off.

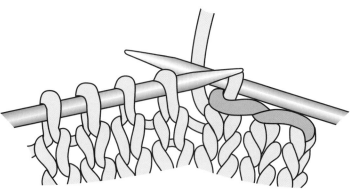

Repeat Step 2 four times more; now knit each of the remaining stitches on the left needle. You should have 18 stitches on the right needle and you have bound off 6 stitches on the knit side of your work. (**Note:** *The first of the 18 stitches was worked while binding off the last stitch at the beginning of the row.*)

To bind off on the purl side, turn your practice piece so the wrong side of your work is facing you.

Purl Bind-Off

Step 1:

Purl the first 2 stitches. Now insert the left needle into the first stitch on the right needle,

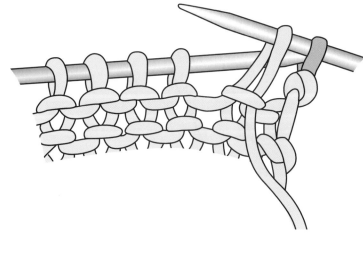

and pull it over the second stitch and completely off the needle. You have now bound off one stitch.

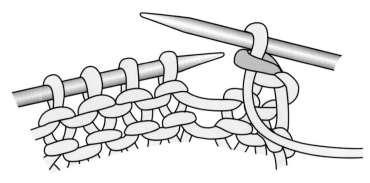

Step 2:

Purl one more stitch; insert the left needle into the first stitch on the right needle and pull the first stitch over the new stitch and completely off the needle. Another stitch is bound off.

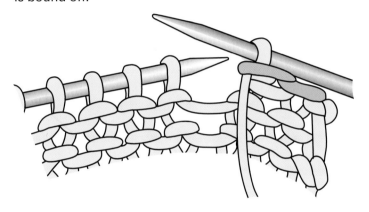

Repeat Step 2 four times more; now purl each of the 11 stitches remaining on the left needle for a total of 12 stitches on the right needle.

Turn your work so that the right side is facing you; bind off 6 stitches in the same manner that you bound off the first 6 stitches on this side, then knit remaining stitches.

Turn your work and bind off the remaining stitches on the wrong side; there will be one stitch left on the needle and you are ready to "finish off" or "end off" the yarn. To do this, cut the yarn leaving about a 6-inch end. With the needle, draw this end up through the final stitch to secure it.

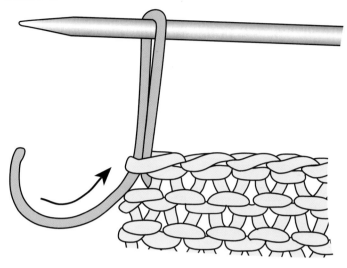

You have just learned to bind off knit stitches on the right side of your work and purl stitches on the wrong side of your work. When you wish to bind off in a pattern stitch, where some stitches in a row have been knitted and others purled, knit the knit stitches and purl the purl stitches as you work across the row.

Always bind off loosely to maintain the same amount of stretch or "give" at the edge as in the rest of your work. If the bind off is too tight at the neckband ribbing of a pullover sweater, for example, the sweater will not fit over your head!

Hint: *You can insure the binding off being loose enough if you replace the needle in your right hand with a needle one size larger.*

Increasing

To shape knitted pieces, you will make them wider or narrower by increasing or decreasing a certain number of stitches from time to time.

Begin a new practice piece by casting on 12 stitches. Work 4 rows of garter stitch (remember this means you will knit every row); then on the next row, purl across (this purl side now becomes the wrong side of the work, since you will now begin working in stockinette stitch). Knit one more row, then purl one more row. You are now ready to practice increasing.

Although there are many ways to increase, this is used most often.

Knit (or Purl) 2 stitches in One

On your practice piece (with the right side facing you), work as follows in the first stitch:

Step 1:

Insert the tip of the right needle from front to back into the stitch, and knit it in the usual manner but don't remove the stitch from the left needle.

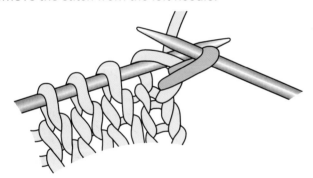

Step 2:

Insert the needle (from front to back) into the back loop of the same stitch, and knit it again, this time slipping the stitch off the left needle. You have now increased one stitch.

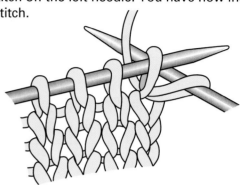

Knit across the row until one stitch remains, then increase again by repeating Steps 1 and 2. You should now have 14 stitches.

Purl one row then knit one row, without increasing.

On your next row, the purl side, again increase in the first stitch. To increase on the purl side, insert the needle from back to front into the stitch; purl the stitch in the usual manner but don't remove it from the left needle. Then insert the needle (from back to front) into the back loop of the same stitch;

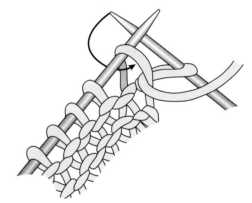

purl it again, this time slipping the stitch off. Then purl across to the last stitch; increase again. You should now have 16 stitches.

Now knit one row and purl one row, without increasing.

Decreasing

Method 1: Right Slanting Decrease

Knit (or Purl) 2 Stitches Together

In this method, you simply knit 2 stitches as one. Knit the first stitch on your practice piece, then decrease as follows:

Step 1:

Insert the needle in usual manner but through the fronts of the next 2 stitches on the left needle.

Step 2:

Bring yarn under and over the point of the needle,

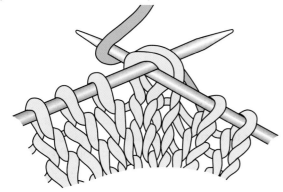

draw the yarn through both stitches,

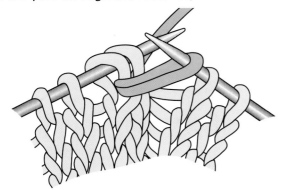

slip the stitches off the left needle and one new stitch will be on the right needle.

You have decreased one stitch. Knit across to the last 3 stitches; repeat Steps 1 and 2 again to decrease another stitch, then knit the last stitch. You should now have 14 stitches.

This decrease can also be worked on the purl side. On the next row of your practice piece, purl 1 stitch, then insert the needle in the fronts of next 2 stitches and purl them as if they were one stitch. Purl to the last 3 stitches, decrease again; purl remaining stitch.

Method 2: Left Slanting Decrease

Pass Slipped Stitch Over

This method is often used in the shaping of raglans or other pieces where a definite decrease line is desired. In the following samples the decrease is worked one stitch in from the edge. By working in one stitch from the edge, the decrease does not become a part of the seam.

To use this method you must first know how to "slip" a stitch. When instructions say to slip a stitch, this means you will slip it from the left needle to the right, without working it. To do this, insert right needle into the stitch as if you were going to purl it (even if it's a knit stitch); but instead of purling, slip the stitch from the left needle to the right needle.

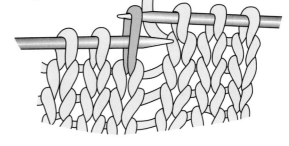

Note: *Always insert the needle as to purl when slipping a stitch, unless instructions specify "slip as to knit"; in that case, insert the needle in the position for knitting, and slip the stitch in the same manner.*

Now that you know how to slip a stitch, you can practice the second method of decreasing. On your practice piece, knit the first stitch. Instructions to decrease may read: "Slip 1, knit 1, pass slipped stitch over." To do this, work as follows.

Step 1:

Slip the next stitch, as to purl.

Step 2:

Knit the next stitch.

Step 3:

Pass the slipped stitch over the knitted stitch by using point of the left needle to lift the slipped stitch over the next stitch and completely off the needle.

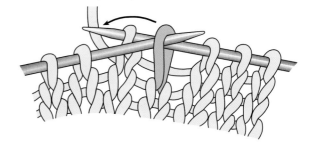

Knit to the last three stitches. Repeat Steps 1, 2 and 3. Then knit the last stitch.

This decrease can also be worked on the purl side. To do so, purl the first stitch. Slip next stitch, purl the next stitch, pass slipped stitch over purled stitch. Purl to the last 3 stitches, then repeat the purl decrease and purl the last stitch.

Hint: *When slipping stitches the yarn is not moved unless specified in the instructions.*

Decreasing, Alternate Method 2: Left Slanting Decrease

Slip, Slip, Knit

This decrease is similar in appearance to the previous method but has a smoother look as the stitch is not lifted or pulled up causing a slightly larger loop.

When this decrease is used the stitches are slipped as if to **knit** *(see Note above).*

To practice this method, knit the first stitch, slip the next two stitches one at a time from the left to the right needle as if to knit.

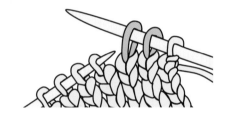

Insert the left needle into the front of both stitches, bring the yarn around the needle as if knitting and lift the 2 stitches over and off the needle at the same time.

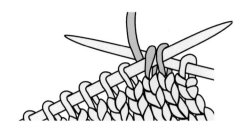

Knit to the last 3 stitches, repeat the slip, slip, knit the 2 slipped stitches together, then knit the last stitch. Purl one row.

Notice the two methods of decreasing. Method 1 causes the decreased stitch to slant from left to right, while in Method 2 the stitch slants from right to left. For a sweater both methods are often used in the same row for a mirrored effect.

To practice this mirrored look, knit 1 stitch, decrease using either of the Method 2 decreases, knit to the last 3 stitches, knit 2 stitches together using Method 1 and knit the last stitch. Notice that both decreases slant towards the center of your sample.

You may continue to practice these methods or if you feel comfortable with them, bind off your sample piece.

Take a break and stretch.

Lesson 8

Ribbing

Sometimes you want a piece of knitting to fit more closely—such as at the neck, wrists or bottom of a sweater. To do this, a combination of knit and purl stitches alternating in the same row, called ribbing, creates an elastic effect. To practice ribbing, start a new piece by casting on 24 stitches loosely. Always cast on for ribbing loosely, to provide enough stretch in the first row.

Knit 2, Purl 2 Ribbing

Pattern Row: Knit 2 stitches, then bring yarn under the needle to the front of the work and purl 2 stitches; take the yarn under the needle to the back of the work and knit 2 stitches; yarn to front again, purl 2 stitches.

Note: *You may tend to add stitches accidentally by forgetting to move the yarn to the front before purling, or to the back before knitting.*

Remembering to move the yarn, repeat this knit 2, purl 2 alternating pattern across the row.

Work this same Pattern Row 11 more times or until you feel comfortable with it. Your work should look like this.

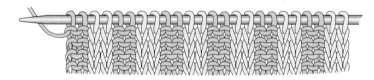

Hint: *If you have trouble distinguishing a knit stitch or a purl stitch, remember that the smooth "v-shaped" stitches are knit stitches and the bumpy ones are purl stitches.*

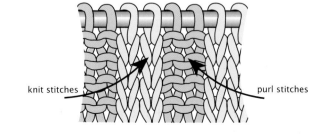

knit stitches   purl stitches

Bind off loosely, remembering to knit the knit stitches and purl the purl stitches. Look at the work and see how the ribbing draws it in.

Knit 1, Purl 1 Ribbing

This rib stitch pattern produces a finer ribbing, and is often used on baby clothes or on garments knitted with light weight yarns.

Again cast on 24 stitches.

Pattern Row: Knit the first stitch, yarn under needle to front, purl the next stitch; yarn under needle to back, knit next stitch; yarn to front, purl next stitch. Continue across row, alternating one knit stitch with one purl stitch.

Work this same Pattern Row 11 more times or until you feel comfortable with this rib pattern. Your work should look like this.

Practice this ribbing for several more rows, then bind off in ribbing, knitting the knit (smooth) stitches and purling the purl (bumpy) stitches.

Changing Yarn

Joining Yarn

New yarn should be added only at the beginning of a row, never in the middle of a row, unless this is required for a color pattern change. To add yarn, tie the new strand around the old strand, making a knot at the edge of work, leaving at least a 4-inch end on both old and new strands. Then proceed to knit with the new yarn. The ends will be hidden later.

Carrying Yarn

When a yarn is repeated every several rows, it can be carried along the edge when not in use. At the beginning of the row, bring the carried color under and over the color just used and begin knitting (or purling).

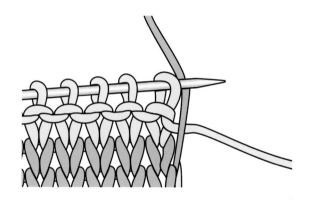

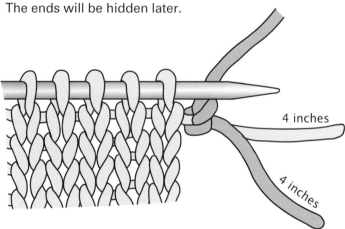

4 inches

4 inches

Gauge and Measuring

This is the most important lesson of all, for if you don't work to gauge, your knitted garments will not fit as designed.

Gauge simply means the number of stitches per inch, and the number of rows per inch, that result from a specified yarn worked with needles in a specified size. This was the information used by the designer when creating the project.

But since everyone knits differently—some loosely, some tightly, some in between—the measurements of individual work will vary greatly, even when the knitters use exactly the same pattern and exactly the same size yarn and needles.

That's why you need to knit a gauge swatch before you start actually working on a project.

Needle sizes given in instructions are merely guides, and should never be used without making a 4-inch square sample swatch to check your gauge. *It is your responsibility to make sure you achieve the gauge specified in the pattern.* To achieve this gauge, you may need to use a different needle size—either larger or smaller—than that specified in the pattern. Always change to larger or smaller needles if necessary to achieve gauge.

Here's how to check your gauge. At the beginning of every knit pattern you'll find a gauge given, like this (note the use of abbreviations):

Gauge

16 sts and 24 rows = 4 inches/10cm in stockinette st, with size 8 needles

This means that you will work your gauge swatch in stockinette stitch, and will try to achieve a gauge of 16 stitches and 24 rows to 4 inches. You must make a gauge swatch at least 4 inches square to adequately test your work.

Starting with the recommended size 8 needle, cast on 16 stitches. Work in stockinette stitch for 24 rows. Loosely bind off all stitches.

Place the swatch on a flat surface and pin it out, being careful not to stretch it. Measure the outside edges; the swatch should be 4 inches square.

Now measure the center 2 inches from side to side, and count the actual stitches. There should be 8 stitches in the 2 inches.

Then measure the center 2 inches from top to bottom and count the rows per inch. There should be 12 rows in the 2 inches.

If you have more stitches or rows per inch than specified, make another swatch with a size larger needles.

If you have fewer stitches or rows per inch than specified, make another swatch with a size smaller needles.

Making gauge swatches before beginning a garment takes time and is a bother. But if you don't make the effort to do this important step, you'll never be able to create attractive, well-fitting garments.

Once you've begun a garment, it's a good idea to keep checking your gauge every few inches; if you become relaxed, you may find yourself knitting more loosely; if you tense up, your knitting may become tighter. To keep your gauge, it may be necessary to change needle sizes in the middle of a garment.

For a swatch in garter stitch, every 2 rows form a ridge which needs to be taken into consideration when counting rows.

Hint: *Sometimes you'll find that you have the correct stitch gauge, but can't get the row gauge even with a change in needle size. If so, the stitch gauge is more important than the row gauge, with one exception: raglan sweaters. In knitting raglans, the armhole depth is based on row gauge, so you must achieve both stitch and row gauge.*

Reading Patterns

Knitting patterns are written in a special language, full of abbreviations, asterisks, parentheses, and other symbols and terms. These short forms are used so instructions will not take up too much space. They may seem confusing at first, but once understood, it is easy to follow them.

Symbols

[ ] work instructions within brackets as many times as directed such as [k2, p2] twice.

* repeat instructions following the * as directed; thus, "rep from * twice" means after working the instructions once, repeat the instructions following the asterisk twice more (3 times in all).

( ) parentheses are used to list the garment sizes and to provide additional information to clarify instructions.

Terms

Right or Wrong?

These words are used in several different ways.

Right Side of the garment means the side that will be seen when it is worn.

Wrong Side of the garment means the side that will be inside when it is worn.

Right-Hand Side means the side of the work closest to your right hand as you are are working on it.

Left-Hand Side means the side of the work closest to your left hand as you are working on it.

Right Shoulder means the part of the garment that will be worn on the right shoulder.

Left Shoulder means the part of the garment that will be worn on the left shoulder.

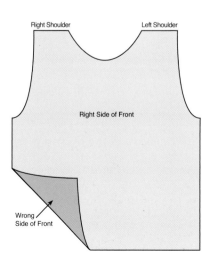

Right Shoulder   Left Shoulder

Right Side of Front

Wrong Side of Front

Work in pattern as established is usually used when referring to a pattern stitch. The term means to continue following the pattern stitch as it is set up (established) on the needle. Work any subsequent increases or decreases in such a way that the established pattern remains the same (usually, working added stitches at the beginning or end of a row), outside the established pattern area.

Work even means to continue to work in the pattern as established, without working any increases or decreases.

Following Size in Patterns

The patterns for garments include a variety of sizes. Each pattern is written for the smallest size pattern with changes in the number of stitches (or inches) for other sizes in parentheses. For example, the pattern will tell you how many stitches to cast on as follows:

Cast on 20 (23, 24) stitches.

You would cast on 20 stitches for the small size, 23 stitches for the medium size and 24 stitches for the large size. Depending on the pattern there may be more sizes or fewer sizes given. Check the measurements to determine the best size to make.

It is helpful before you begin knitting to highlight or circle all the numbers throughout the pattern for the size you are making.

Abbreviations

approx .... approximately	rem .... remain/remaining
beg .... begin/beginning	rep .... repeat(s)
CC .... contrasting color	RH .... right hand
cm .... centimeter(s)	rnd(s) .... rounds
dec .... decrease(s)/decreasing	RS .... right side
g .... gram	sl .... slip
inc .... increase(s)/increasing	sl 1k .... slip 1 knitwise
k .... knit	sl 1p .... slip 1 purlwise
k2tog .... knit 2 stitches together	sl st(s) .... slip stitch(es)
LH .... left hand	ssk .... slip, slip, knit these
lp(s) .... loop(s)	2 stitches together—a decrease
m .... meter(s)	st(s) .... stitch(es)
M1 .... make one stitch	St st .... stockinette stitch
MC .... main color	tbl .... through back loop(s)
mm .... millimeter(s)	tog .... together
oz .... ounce(s)	WS .... wrong side
p .... purl	wyib .... with yarn in back
pat(s) .... pattern(s)	wyif .... with yarn in front
p2tog .... purl 2 stitches together	yd(s) .... yard(s)
psso .... pass slipped stitch over	YO .... yarn over

Finishing

Many a well-knitted garment, worked exactly to gauge, ends up looking sloppy and amateurish, simply because of bad finishing. To finish a knitted garment requires no special skill, but it does require time, attention and a knowledge of basic techniques.

Picking up Stitches

You will often need to pick up a certain number of stitches along an edge, such as around a sweater neckline or armhole, so that ribbing or an edging can be worked. The pattern instructions will usually state clearly where and how many stitches to pick up. Although this is not difficult, it is often done incorrectly and the results look messy. Many times a circular needle is used for picking up stitches. For a neck edge, once the stitches are picked up, you begin knitting again in the first stitch and continue to work around the needle until the desired length is achieved.

To pick up a stitch, hold the knitting with the right side of the work facing you. Hold yarn from the skein behind the work, and hold a knitting needle in your right hand. Insert the point of the needle into the work from front to back, one stitch (at least 2 threads) from the edge; wrap the yarn around the needle as if knitting and draw the yarn through with the needle to the right side of the work making one stitch on the needle.

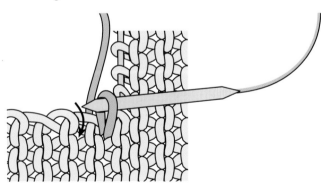

Pick up another stitch in the same manner, spacing stitches evenly along the edge.

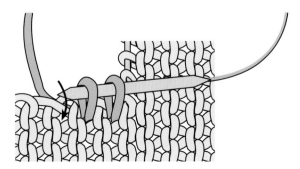

When picking up, pick up one stitch for each stitch when working across stitches in a horizontal row, and pick up about 3 stitches for every 4 rows when working along end of rows. If a large number of stitches are to be picked up, it is best to mark off the edge into equal sections, then pick up the same number of stitches in each section.

For stitches that have been bound-off along a neck edge, pick up through both loops of each stitch.

Sometimes stitches are placed on a holder when working the front and back of a garment. When picking up these stitches they can either be knit directly from the holder or slipped to another needle and knit from it, depending on how they were originally slipped onto the holder.

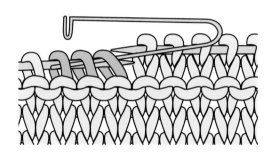

Blocking

Blocking simply means "setting" each piece into its final size and shape. (**Note:** *Be sure to check the yarn label before blocking, as some synthetic yarns and mohair yarns are ruined if they are blocked.*)

To block, moisten each piece first by dampening it with a light water spray. Then place each piece out on a padded flat surface (terry toweling provides adequate padding) right side up and away from direct sunlight. Referring to the small drawing or schematic in the pattern for the measurements for each piece, smooth out each piece to correct size and shape, using your fingers and the palms of your hands. Be sure to keep the stitches and rows in straight alignment. Use rust-proof straight pins to hold the edges in place. Let pieces dry completely before removing.

If further blocking is required, use steam from a steam iron. Hold the iron close to the knitted piece and allow the steam to penetrate the fabric. Never rest the iron directly on the piece—knitting should never have a pressed flat look. Let dry completely before removing.

Important Note: *Never press ribbing, garter stitch, cables, or textured patterns as in Irish knits.*

Sewing Seams

Your pattern will usually tell you in what order to

assemble the pieces. Use the same yarn as used in the garment to sew the seams, unless the yarn is too thick, in which case use a thinner yarn in a matching color.

Invisible Seam

This seam gives a smooth and neat appearance, as it weaves the edges together invisibly from the right side.

To join horizontal edges, such as shoulder seams, sew the edges together as shown.

To join a front/back vertical edge to a horizontal sleeve edge, weave the edges together as shown.

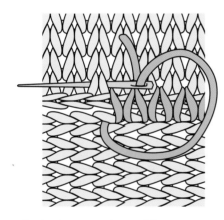

To join vertical edges, such as side seams or underarm sleeve seams, sew the edges together on the right side, pulling yarn gently until the edges meet.

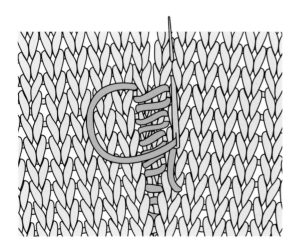

For pieces made using garter stitch join vertical edges as shown.

Hint: *When seaming, do not draw the stitches too tight, as the joining should have the same stretch or give as in the knitted garment.*

Weaving in Ends

The final step is to weave in all the yarn ends securely. To do this, use a size 16 tapestry needle and weave the yarn end through the backs of stitches.

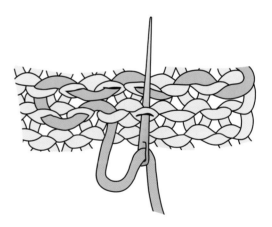

First weave the yarn about 2 inches in one direction and then 1 inch in the reverse direction. Cut off excess yarn.

If the ends are close to a seam weave the yarn back and forth along the edge of the seam.

Congratulations! You've graduated!

Now you've learned the basics of knitting and can go on to make your first project.

Metric Chart

INCHES INTO MILLIMETERS & CENTIMETERS (Rounded off slightly)

inches	mm	cm	inches	cm	inches	cm	inches	cm
1/8	3	0.3	5	12.5	21	53.5	38	96.5
1/4	6	0.6	5 1/2	14	22	56	39	99
3/8	10	1	6	15	23	58.5	40	101.5
1/2	13	1.3	7	18	24	61	41	104
5/8	15	1.5	8	20.5	25	63.5	42	106.5
3/4	20	2	9	23	26	66	43	109
7/8	22	2.2	10	25.5	27	68.5	44	112
1	25	2.5	11	28	28	71	45	114.5
1 1/4	32	3.2	12	30.5	29	73.5	46	117
1 1/2	38	3.8	13	33	30	76	47	119.5
1 3/4	45	4.5	14	35.5	31	79	48	122
2	50	5	15	38	32	81.5	49	124.5
2 1/2	65	6.5	16	40.5	33	84	50	127
3	75	7.5	17	43	34	86.5		
3 1/2	90	9	18	46	35	89		
4	100	10	19	48.5	36	91.5		
4 1/2	115	11.5	20	51	37	94		

KNITTING NEEDLES CONVERSION CHART

U.S.	0	1	2	3	4	5	6	7	8	9	10	10 1/2	11	13	15
Metric(mm)	2	2 1/4	2 3/4	3 1/4	3 1/2	3 3/4	4	4 1/2	5	5 1/2	6	6 1/2	8	9	10

Standard Yarn Weight System

Categories of yarn, gauge ranges, and recommended needle sizes

Yarn Weight Symbol & Category Names	1 SUPER FINE	2 FINE	3 LIGHT	4 MEDIUM	5 BULKY	6 SUPER BULKY
Type of Yarns in Category	Sock, Fingering, Baby	Sport, Baby	DK, Light Worsted	Worsted, Afghan, Aran	Chunky, Craft, Rug	Bulky, Roving
Knit Gauge Range* in Stockinette Stitch to 4 inches	27–32 sts	23–26 sts	21–24 sts	16–20 sts	12–15 sts	6–11 sts
Recommended Needle in Metric Size Range	2.25–3.25 mm	3.25–3.75 mm	3.75–4.5 mm	4.5–5.5 mm	5.5–8 mm	8 mm and larger
Recommended Needle U.S. Size Range	1 to 3	3 to 5	5 to 7	7 to 9	9 to 11	11 and larger

* GUIDELINES ONLY: The above reflect the most commonly used gauges and needle sizes for specific yarn categories.

Fringe

Fringe Instructions

Some of the projects in this book call for fringe to be added. To make fringe, cut a piece of cardboard half as long as specified in instructions for strands plus ½ inch for trimming. Wind yarn loosely and evenly around cardboard. When cardboard is filled, cut yarn across one end. Do this several times then begin adding fringeing. Wind additional strands as necessary.

Hold specified number of strands for one knot together, fold in half. Hold project to be fringed with right side facing you. Use crochet hook to draw folded end through space or stitch indicated from right to wrong side (Figs. 1 and 2).

Pull loose ends through folded section (Fig. 3).

Draw knot up firmly (Fig. 4).

Space knots as indicated in pattern instructions.

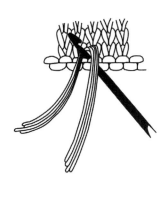

Fig. 1

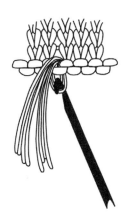

Fig. 2

Fig. 3

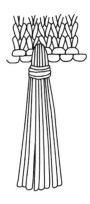

Fig. 4

Skill Levels

◖■☐☐☐ BEGINNER
Beginner projects for first-time crocheters using basic stitches. Minimal shaping.

◖■■☐☐ EASY
Easy projects using basic stitches, repetitive stitch patterns, simple color changes and simple shaping and finishing.

◖■■■☐ INTERMEDIATE
Intermediate projects with a variety of stitches, mid-level shaping and finishing.

◖■■■◗ EXPERIENCED
Experienced projects using advanced techniques and stitches, detailed shaping and refined finishing.

Russian Tea Room Scarf

Design by Kathleen Power Johnson

Skill Level

BEGINNER

Measurements

102 inches long x 3 inches wide

Materials

- Bulky fur-type yarn (1.76 oz/68 yds/50g per ball): 2 balls fever #3375

Note: *Our photographed sample made with Moda Dea Kickx*

- Size 13 (9mm) knitting needle or size needed to obtain gauge

Gauge

12 sts = 3 inches and 16 rows = 4 inches in garter stitch (knit every row)

Exact gauge not critical to this project.

Special Abbreviation

Increase (inc): Inc 1 st by knitting in the front and back of stitch.

Scarf

Beginning Point

Cast on 1 st.

Row 1 (RS): Inc *(see Special Abbreviation).* (2 sts)

Row 2 and all even-numbered rows: Knit.

Row 3: Inc, k1. (3 sts)

Row 5: Inc, k2. (4 sts)

Row 7: Inc, k3. (5 sts)

Row 9: Inc, k4. (6 sts)

Row 11: Inc, k5. (7 sts)

Row 13: Inc, k6. (8 sts)

Row 15: Inc, k7. (9 sts)

Row 17: Inc, k8. (10 sts)

Row 19: Inc, k9. (11 sts)

Row 21: Inc, k10. (12 sts)

Body

Work even in garter stitch until scarf measures 97 inches, or 5 inches less than desired length, ending by working a WS row.

Ending point

Row 1 (RS): K10, k2tog. (11 sts)

Row 2 and all even-numbered rows: Knit.

Row 3: K9, k2tog. (10 sts)

Row 5: K8, k2tog. (9 sts)

Row 7: K7, k2tog. (8 sts)

Row 9: K6, k2tog. (7 sts)

Row 11: K5, k2tog. (6 sts)

Row 13: K4, k2tog. (5 sts)

Row 15: K3, k2tog. (4 sts)

Row 17: K2, k2tog. (3 sts)

Row 17: K2, k2tog. (2 sts)

Row 19: K2tog.

Fasten off.

Greenhorn Scarf

Design by Edie Eckman

Skill Level

EASY

Finished Size

Approx 7½ x 52 inches

Materials

- Bulky weight yarn (6 oz/185 yds/170g per ball): 1 ball Florida Keys green #369

Note: *Our photographed scarf was made with Lion Brand Homespun.*

- Size 11 (8mm) needles or size needed to obtain gauge

Gauge

11 sts = 4 inches/10cm in garter st (knit every row)

Exact gauge is not critical to this project.

Special Abbreviation

Increase (inc): Inc 1 st by knitting in the front and back of stitch.

Pattern Notes

If a longer scarf is desired, a second ball of yarn is needed.

Scarf is reversible.

Scarf

Beginning Diagonal

Cast on 3 sts.

Row 1: Knit.

Row 2: Inc *(see Special Abbreviation),* knit across.

Rep Row 2 until there are 32 sts.

Body

Row 1: Knit.

Row 2: K2tog, knit to last st, inc.

Rep Row 2 until scarf measures approx 52 inches on long side.

Ending Diagonal

Row 1: Knit.

Row 2: K2tog, knit across.

Rep Row 2 until 3 sts rem.

Next Row: Knit.

Bind off and weave in ends.

By George Shaheen

Skill Level

■■□□

EASY

Size

Approx 4½ x 42 inches

Materials

- Medium (worsted) weight glitter yarn (1¾ oz/115 yds/50g per ball): 2 balls ruby #113
- Novelty "eyelash" yarn (1¾ oz/60 yds/50g per ball): 1 ball red #113

Note: *Our photographed scarf was made with Lion Brand Glitterspun, and Lion Brand Fun Fur, Red.*

- Size 15 (10mm) knitting needles
- Size 17 (12.75mm) knitting needles or size needed to obtain gauge
- Tapestry needle

Gauge

14 sts = 4½ inches in pattern stitch with larger size needles and one strand of each yarn held together

Exact gauge is not critical to this project.

Pattern Note

Scarf is reversible.

Scarf

With smaller needles and two strands of glitter yarn held together, cast on 14 sts.

Row 1: K2; *p2, k2; rep from * twice more.

Row 2: P2; *k2, p2; rep from * twice more.

Rep Rows 1 and 2 until piece measures 4 inches from cast-on edge. Cut one strand of glitter yarn.

Change to larger needles.

With one strand of each yarn held together, continue in pattern as established until piece measures 38 inches from cast-on edge. Cut novelty yarn.

Change to smaller needles.

With two strands of glitter yarn held together, continue in pattern until piece measures 42 inches from cast-on edge.

Bind off in pattern.

Scarf Rings

Make 2

With smaller needles and two strands of glitter yarn held together, cast on 4 sts.

Row 1 (RS): P1, k2, p1.

Row 2: K1, p2, k1.

Rows 3–8: [Rep Rows 1 and 2] 3 times more.

Bind off.

Finishing

For scarf ring, with RS facing, sew bound-off edge to cast-on edge to form ring.

Rep for other ring.

Slide end of scarf through scarf ring to first row of novelty yarn; tack in place to hold.

Rep with other ring on opposite edge of scarf.

Perfectly Pink Scarf & Hat

Design by Kathy Wesley

Skill Level

EASY

Size

Hat: Child small (child medium, child large, adult)

Scarf: Child (adult)

Instructions are given for smallest size, with larger sizes in parentheses. When only 1 number is given, it applies to all sizes.

Finished Measurements

Hat: 19 (20, 21, 22) inch head circumference

Scarf: 2½ x 54 inches (5 x 73 inches)

Materials

For Hat:

- Worsted weight yarn (3.5 oz/174 yds/100g per ball): 2 balls grenadine #730 (MC); 1 ball each cornmeal #220 (A), medium coral #252 (B) and lavender #584 (C)

Note: *1 ball each of A, B and C sufficient for both hat and scarf*

For Scarf:

- Worsted weight yarn (3.5oz/174 yds/100g per skein) 2 skeins grenadine #730 (MC)

Note: *Our photographed hat and scarf were made with Red Heart Classic.*

- Size 8 (5mm) knitting needles (for hat only)
- Size 9 (5.5mm) knitting needles or size needed to obtain gauge
- Tapestry needle
- Size G/8/5mm crochet hook (for attaching tassel)

Gauge

16 sts and 32 rows = 4 inches/10cm in garter st (knit every row)

To save time, take time to check gauge.

Special Abbreviation

Increase (inc): Inc 1 st by knitting in front and back of st.

Hat

Border

With smaller needles and MC, cast on 64 (68, 72, 76) sts.

Row 1 (RS): *K1, p1; rep from * across.

Rows 2–6: Rep Row 1.

Change to larger needles.

Body

Rows 1 and 2: With A, knit.

Rows 3 and 4: With B, knit.

Rows 5 and 6: With C, knit. Fasten off all colors.

Row 7: With MC, *k15 (16, 17,18), **inc** (see Special Abbreviation); rep from * 3 times more. (68, 72, 76, 80 sts)

With MC, work in garter st until piece measures 5 (5½, 6, 7) inches from cast-on edge, ending by working a WS row.

Shaping

Row 1 (RS): K14 (15, 16, 17), k2tog; *k15 (16, 17, 18), k2 tog; rep from * twice more; k1. (64, 68, 72, 76 sts)

Rows 2–4: Knit.

Row 5: K13 (14, 15, 16), k2tog; *k14 (15, 16, 17), k2tog; rep from * twice more; k1. (60, 64, 68, 72 sts)

Rows 6–8: Knit.

Row 9: K12 (13, 14, 15) sts, k2tog; *k13 (14, 15, 16), k2tog; rep from * twice more, k1. (56, 60, 64, 68 sts)

Rows 10 and 12: Knit.

Row 13: K11 (12, 13, 14), k2tog; *k12 (13, 14, 15), k2tog; rep from * twice more, k1. (52, 56, 60, 64 sts)

Rows 14–16: Knit.

Row 17: K10 (11, 12, 13), k2tog; *k11 (12, 13, 14), k2tog; rep from * twice more, k1. (48, 52, 56, 60 sts)

Rows 18–20: Knit.

Row 21: K9 (10, 11, 12), k2tog; *k10 (11, 12, 13), k2tog; rep from * twice more, k1. (44, 48, 52, 56 sts)

Rows 22–24: Knit.

Row 25: K8 (9, 10, 11), k2tog; *k9 (10, 11, 12), k2tog; rep from * twice more; k1. (40, 44, 48, 52 sts)

Rows 26–28: Knit.

Row 29: K7 (8, 9, 10), k2tog; *k8 (9, 10, 11), k2tog; rep from * twice more; k1. (36, 40, 44, 48 sts)

Rows 30–32: Knit.

Row 33: K6 (7, 8, 9), k2tog; *k7 (8, 9, 10), k2tog; rep from * twice more; k1. (32, 36, 40, 44 sts)

Rows 34–36: Knit.

Row 37: K5 (6, 7, 8), k2tog; *k6 (7, 8, 9), k2tog; rep from * twice more; k1. (28, 32, 36, 40 sts)

Rows 38–40: Knit.

Continue working in garter st, dec on next and every 4th row in same manner and having one less st between dec until 8 sts rem.

Cut yarn, leaving a 24-inch length. With tapestry needle weave yarn through rem sts and pull tight.

Finishing

Sew side edges tog carefully matching rows.

Cut two 8-inch lengths each of A, B and C. Hold strands together and fold in half. With crochet hook, draw folded end through peak of hat. Pull loose ends through folded section and draw knot up firmly. Trim ends evenly.

Scarf

Note: Stripe sequence on second end is worked in reverse order so appearance is the same when scarf is worn.

First End

With larger needles and MC, cast on 10 (20) sts.

Row 1 (RS): Knit.

Rows 2–4: Knit.

Rows 5 and 6: With A, knit.

Rows 7 and 8: With B, knit.

Rows 9 and 10: With C, knit.

Rows 11–30: With MC, knit.

[Rep Rows 5–30] 3 (5) times more.

Rep Rows 5–10 once.

Body

With MC, knit until scarf measures 40 (50) inches, ending by working a WS row.

Second End

Rows 1 (RS) and 2: With C, knit.

Rows 3 and 4: With B, knit.

Rows 5 and 6: With A, knit.

Rows 7–26: With MC, knit.

[Rep Rows 1–26] 3 (5) times more.

Rep Rows 1–6 once more.

With MC knit 3 rows.

Bind off.

Weave in all ends.

Design by Sandy Scoville

Skill Level

BEGINNER

Size

Approx 18 inches square

Materials

- Bulky weight yarn (6 oz/108 yds/170g per ball): 3 balls wheat #402

Note: *Our photographed pillow was made with Lion Brand Wool-Ease Thick & Quick.*
- Size 10½ (6.5mm) knitting needles or size needed to obtain gauge
- Tapestry needle
- 18-inch square knife-edge pillow form

Gauge

10 sts = 4 inches/10cm in stockinette st (knit one row, purl one row)

To save time, take time to check gauge.

Pillow

Front/Back

Make 2 alike

Cast on 45 sts.

Row 1 (RS): K5, *p3, k5; rep from * across.

Row 2: P5, *k3, p3; rep from * across.

Rows 3 and 4: Rep Rows 1 and 2.

Row 5: K1, p3, *k5, p3; rep from * 5 times more; k1.

Row 6: P1, k3, *p5, k3; rep from * 5 times more, p1.

Rows 7 and 8: Rep Rows 5 and 6.

Rows 9–72: [Rep Rows 1–8] 8 times more.

Bind off as to purl.

Finishing

Hold front and back pieces with RS tog and one side edge at top; sew along side edge, across top edge and along next side.

Turn right side out. Insert pillow form and sew remaining edge.

Design by Sandy Scoville

Skill Level

BEGINNER

Size

About 11 x 9 inches

Materials

- Worsted weight cotton yarn: (2 oz/95 yds/56g per ball): 1 ball cool breeze ombre #00227 **or** (2.5 oz/120 yds/70g per ball): 1 ball yellow #0010

MEDIUM 4

Note: *Our photographed dishcloths were made with Lily Sugar 'n Cream*

- Size 8 (5mm) knitting needles or size needed to obtain gauge

Gauge

18 sts = 4 inches/10cm in stockinette st (knit one row, purl one row)

To save time, take time to check gauge.

Dishcloth

Lower Border

Cast on 50 sts.

Row 1 (RS): Knit.

Rows 2–6: Knit.

Body

Row 1 (RS): K4, p2, *k3, p2; rep from * 8 times more; k4.

Row 2: K6, *p1, k1, p1, k2; rep from * 8 times more; k4.

Rep Rows 1 and 2 until piece measures about 9½ inches from cast-on edge, ending with a Row 2.

Upper Border

Row 1 (RS): Knit.

Rows 2–5: Knit.

Bind off.

Wrapped-in-Warmth Shawl

Design by Scarlet Taylor

Skill Level

BEGINNER

Finished Measurements

Approx 24 x 72 inches (excluding fringe)

Materials

- Bulky weight yarn (1.75 oz/55 yds/50g per ball): 15 balls pastel meadows #540-272

Note: Our photographed shawl was made with Lion Brand Landscapes.

- Size 11 (8mm) knitting needles
- Size 13 (9mm) knitting needles or size needed to obtain gauge
- Size J/10/6mm crochet hook (for fringe)

Gauge

11 sts and 14 rows = 4 inches/10cm in stockinette st with larger needles

To save time, take time to check gauge.

Shawl

With smaller needles, cast on 66 sts.

Lower edging

Rows 1–4: Knit.

Change to larger needles.

Body

Row 1 (RS): Knit.

Row 2: K2, purl to last 2 sts, k2.

Rep Rows 1 and 2 until piece measures approx 71 inches from beg, ending with a RS row.

Change to smaller needles.

Upper edging

Knit 4 rows.

Bind off knitwise.

Weave in ends.

Fringe

Referring to Fringe instructions on page 21, make fringe. Cut 16-inch lengths of yarn. Use 4 strands for each knot. Tie knots evenly spaced (about every third st) across each short end of shawl. Trim end evenly.

Kaleidoscope Throw

Design by George Shaheen

Skill Level

◼️◻️◻️◻️

BEGINNER

Finished Size

Approx 45 inches square

Materials

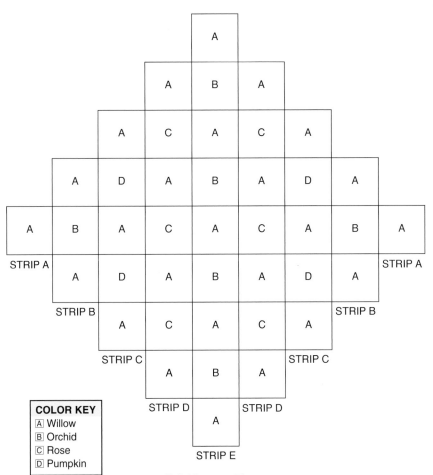

- Bulky weight yarn (5 oz/153 yds/140g per ball): 3 skeins willow #173 (A), 2 skeins evergreen #180 (E), and 1 skein each of orchid #146 (B), pumpkin #133 (D) and deep rose #140 (C)

Note: *Our photographed throw was made with Lion Brand Wool-Ease Chunky.*

- Size 11 (8mm) knitting needles, or size needed to obtain gauge
- Tapestry needle
- 6-inch piece of cardboard

Gauge

11 sts and 20 rows = 4 inches in garter stitch (knit every row)

To save time, take time to check gauge.

Strip A

Make 2

With A, cast on 14 sts.

Rows 1–24: Knit.

Bind off.

Strip B

Make 2

With A cast on 14 sts.

Rows 1–24: Knit. At end of Row 24, cut A.

Rows 25–48: With B, knit. At end of Row 48, cut B.

Rows 49–72: With A, knit.

Bind off.

Strip C

Make 2

With A, cast on 14 sts.

Rows 1–24: Knit. At end of Row 24, cut A.

Rows 25–48: With D, knit. At end of Row 48, cut D.

Rows 49–72: With A, knit. At end of Row 72, A.

Rows 73–96: With D, knit. At end of Row 72, cut D.

Rows 97–120: With A, knit.

Bind off.

Strip D

Make 2

With A, cast on 14 sts.

Rows 1–24: Knit. At end of Row 24, cut A.

Rows 25–48: With C, knit. At end of Row 48, cut C.

Rows 49–72: With A, knit. At end of Row 72, cut A.

Rows 73–96: With C, knit. At end of Row 96, cut C.

Rows 97–120: With A, knit. At end of Row 120, cut A.

Rows 121–144: With C, knit. At end of Row 144, cut C.

Row 145–168: With A, knit.

Bind off.

Strip E

Make 1

With A, cast on 14 sts.

Rows 1–24: Knit. At end of Row 24, cut A.

Rows 25–48: With B, knit. At end of Row 48, cut B.

Rows 49–72: With A, knit. At end of Row 72, cut A.

Rows 73–96: With B, knit. At end of Row 96, cut B.

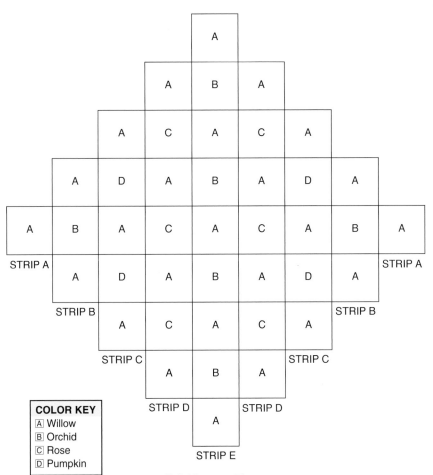

COLOR KEY
- A Willow
- B Orchid
- C Rose
- D Pumpkin

Kaleidoscope Throw

Rows 97–120: With A, knit. At end of Row 120, cut A.

Rows 121–144: With B, knit. At end of Row 144, cut B.

Row 145–168: With A, knit. At end of Row 168, cut A.

Rows 169–192: With B, knit. At end of Row 192, cut B.

Rows 193–216: With A, knit. Bind off.

Finishing

Referring to Assembly Diagram for placement, with A, sew strips together.

Tassel

Make 20

Cut one 12-inch length of E and place it across top of 6-inch length of cardboard. Wrap E 18 times around cardboard over strand at top. Tie 12-inch length tightly at top of tassel, leaving ends for finishing. Cut ends at bottom and remove from cardboard. Cut 16-inch length of E and tie it twice around tassel about 1 inch from top. With lengths left for finishing, tie tassel at one outer edge point. Trim ends even.

Good-bye Goosebumps Poncho

Design by Kathy Wesley

Child

Skill Level

BEGINNER

Size

Child's 6 (8, 10) Instructions are given for smallest size, with larger sizes in parentheses. When only 1 number is given, it applies to all sizes.

Materials

- Super bulky yarn (115 yds/85g per ball): 2 (2, 3) balls seaspray #9381 **SUPER BULKY**

Note: *Our photographed poncho was made with TLC Macaroon.*

- Size 11 (8mm) needles or size needed to obtain gauge

Gauge

9 sts = 4 inches/10cm in garter st (knit every row)

To save time, take time to check gauge.

Special Abbreviation

Kw2: Knit next stitch, wrapping yarn twice around needle.

Pattern Note

Poncho is worked in 2 rectangular pieces then sewn together.

Front/Back

Make 2 alike
Cast on 38 (44, 50) sts.

Row 1 (RS): Knit.

Rows 2–4: Knit.

Row 5: K1, *kw2 *(see Special Abbreviations);* rep from * to last st, k1.

Row 6: K1; *knit, dropping extra wrap; rep from * to last st, k1.

Rows 7 and 8: Knit.

[Rep Rows 5–8] 4 (5, 7) times more.

Next row: Knit.
Bind off loosely knitwise.

Finishing

Referring to diagram block pieces to measurements. Sew pieces together as indicated.

Adult

Skill Level

BEGINNER

Size

One size fits most

Materials

- Super bulky yarn (115 yds/85g per ball): 3 balls pink violet #9351 **SUPER BULKY**

Note: *Our photographed poncho was made with TLC Macaroon.*

- Size 11 (8mm) needles or size needed to obtain gauge

Gauge

10 sts = 4 inches/10cm in garter st (knit every row)

To save time, take time to check gauge.

Special Abbreviation

Kw2: Knit next stitch, wrapping yarn twice around needle.

Pattern Note

Poncho is worked in 2 rectangular pieces then sewn together.

Front/Back

Make 2 alike
Cast on 62 sts.

Row 1 (RS): Knit.

Rows 2–4: Knit.

Row 5: K1, *kw2 *(see Special Abbreviations);* rep from * to last st, k1.

Row 6: K1; *knit, dropping extra wrap; rep from * to last st, k1.

Rows 7 and 8: Knit.

[Rep Rows 5–8] 10 times.

Next row: Knit.

Bind off loosely knitwise.

Finishing

Block pieces to measure 14 x 28 inches.

Sew pieces together as indicated on diagram using largest set of numbers.

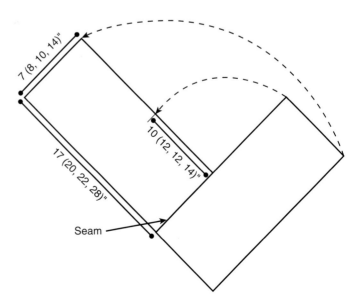

7 (8, 10, 14)"

10 (12, 12, 14)"

17 (20, 22, 28)"

Seam

Goodbye Goosebumps Poncho

Design by Kathy Wesley

Skill Level

EASY

Finished Size

Approx 36 x 42 inches (excluding fringe)

Materials

- Sport weight yarn (6 oz/509 yds/170g per skein): 3 skeins sky blue #7812 (A) and 1 skein white #5011 (B)

Note: *Our photographed afghan was made with TLC Baby.*

- Size 6 (4mm) 36-inch circular needle or size needed to obtain gauge

Gauge

20 sts = 4 inches/10cm in stockinette st (knit one row, purl one row)

To save time, take time to check gauge.

Special Abbreviations

Slip (sl): Slip st from left needle to right needle inserting right needle into st as if to purl, unless otherwise stated.

With yarn in front (wyif): Bring yarn from back of work under the needle and hold in front of work while slipping indicated number of sts.

With yarn in back (wyib): Take yarn from front of work under the needle and hold in back of work while slipping indicated number of sts.

Pattern Notes

Circular needle is used to accommodate large number of stitches. Do not join; work back and forth in rows.

Carry color not in use loosely along edge of afghan. At beg of row bring the working color under the previous color to lock it in place.

Afghan

With A, cast on 185 sts.

Row 1 (RS): Knit.

Row 2: Purl. Drop A.

Row 3: With B, k4, *sl 3 *(see Special Abbreviations)* **wyif** *(see Special Abbreviations)*, k3 **wyib** *(see Special Abbreviations)*; rep from * to last st, end k1.

Row 4: P4, *sl 3 wyib, p3 wyif; rep from * to last st, p1. Drop B.

Row 5: With A, knit.

Row 6: Purl.

Row 7: K5, *insert RH needle under 2 strands of B and into next st on LH needle as if to knit, knit st and bring strands over needle, k5; rep from * across.

Row 8: Purl. Drop A.

Row 9: With B, k1, *sl 3 wyif, k3 wyib; rep from * to last 4 sts, end sl 3 wyif, k1 wyib.

Row 10: P1, *sl 3 wyib, p3 wyif; rep from * to last 4 sts, end sl 3 wyib, p1 wyif. Drop white.

Row 11: With A, knit.

Row 12: Purl.

Row 13: K2, *insert RH needle under 2 strands of B and into next st on LH needle, knit st bringing strands over needle, k5; rep from * to last 3 sts, insert RH needle under 2 strands of B and into next st on LH needle, knit st and bring strands over needle, k2.

Row 14: Purl. Drop A.

[Rep Rows 3–14] 29 times more.

Rep Rows 3–7.

Bind off purlwise.

Fringe

Referring to fringe instructions on page 21 make fringe. Cut 20-inch lengths of A. For each knot use 6 strands. Tie knots evenly spaced (about every ½ inch) across cast-on edge of afghan. Fringe only cast-on edge of afghan, to avoid having fringe close to baby's face.

Rainbow Ladder

Design by Sandy Scoville

Skill Level

EASY

Size

Approx 42 x 60 inches before fringe

Materials

- Medium (worsted) weight yarn (3 oz/210 yds/90g per skein): 10 skeins blue (MC) and 1 skein each of 7 different colors

Note: *Our photographed afghan was made with one yarn for the main color and 7 assorted colors of scrap yarns.*

- Size 8 (5mm) 29-inch circular knitting needle or size needed to obtain gauge

Gauge

20 sts = 4 inches/10cm in stockinette st (knit one row, purl one row)

To save time, take time to check gauge.

Special Abbreviations

With yarn in back (wyib): Hold yarn in back of work while slipping the indicated number of sts. **Note:** *It may be necessary to move yarn under needle to front of work after slipping sts.*

With yarn in front (wyif): Hold yarn in front of work while slipping the indicated number of sts. **Note:** *It may be necessary to move yarn under needle to back of work after slipping sts.*

Slip (sl): Slip st from left needle to right needle inserting right needle as if to purl, unless otherwise stated.

Pattern Note

Carry MC loosely along side edge when not in use. At beg of row bring the working color under the previous color to lock it in place.

Afghan

With MC, cast on 188 sts.

Bottom Border
Row 1 (RS): Knit.

Rows 2 through 4: Rep Row 1.

Body
Row 1 (RS): With MC, knit.

Row 2: Purl.

Rows 3 and 4: Rep Rows 1 and 2.

Row 5: With any scrap color, k8; ***sl** 2 *(see Special Abbreviations)* **wyib** *(see Special Abbreviations)*, k8; rep from ***** across.

Row 6: K8; *****sl 2 **wyif** *(see Special Abbreviations)*, k8; rep from ***** across.

Row 7: P8; *****sl 2 wyib, p8; rep from ***** across.

Row 8: Rep Row 6.

Rows 9–12: Rep Rows 1–4.

Rows 13–16: With new color, rep Rows 5–8.

Rep Rows 1–8, changing to new color on each Row 5, until afghan measures about 60 inches, ending by working a Row 4.

Top Border
Row 1 (RS): With MC, knit.

Rows 2–5: Rep Row 1.

Bind off.

Weave in all ends.

Fringe

Referring to fringe instructions on page 21 make fringe. Cut 24-inch lengths of MC. For each knot use 8 strands. Tie knots evenly spaced (at each MC stripe and each corner) across each short end of afghan.

Trim ends even.

Dashing Hues

Design by Sandy Scoville

Skill Level

■■□□
EASY

Size

Approx 44 x 62 inches

Materials

- Medium (worsted) weight yarn (3 oz/210 yds/90g per skein): 9 skeins off-white (MC); 2 skeins blue (A); 1 skein each of 5 different colors

Note: *Our photographed afghan was made with one yarn for main color, a second color for the stripe and 5 assorted colors for dashes of color.*

- Size 8 (5mm) 29-inch circular knitting needle or size needed to obtain gauge

Gauge

20 sts = 4 inches/10cm in stockinette st (knit one row, purl one row)

To save time, take time to check gauge.

Special Abbreviations

With yarn in back (wyib): Hold yarn in back of work while slipping the indicated number of sts. **Note:** *It may be necessary to move yarn under needle to front of work after slipping sts.*

With yarn in front (wyif): Hold yarn in front of work while slipping the indicated number of sts. **Note:** *It may be necessary to move yarn under needle to back of work after slipping sts.*

Slip (sl): Slip st from left needle to right needle inserting right needle as if to purl, unless otherwise stated.

Pattern Note

Carry MC loosely along side edge when not in use.

Afghan

With MC, cast on 185 sts.

Bottom Border

Row 1 (RS): Knit.

Rows 2–4: Rep Row 1.

Body

Row 1 (RS): With MC, knit.

Row 2: Purl.

Rows 3 and 4: Rep Rows 1 and 2.

Row 5: With Color A, knit.

Row 6: Knit.

Rows 7–10: With MC, rep Rows 1–4.

Row 11: With any scrap color, k1, sl 3 *(see Special Abbreviations)* **wyib** *(see Special Abbreviations)*, *k3, sl 1 wyib, k3, sl 3 wyib; rep from * to last st; K1.

Row 12: K1, sl 3 **wyif** *(see Special Abbreviations)*, *k3, sl 1 wyif, k3, sl 3 wyif; rep from * to last st; k1.

Rows 13 and 14: With MC, rep Rows 1 and 2.

Rows 15 and 16: With same scrap color, rep Rows 11 and 12.

Rows 17 and 18: With MC, rep Rows 1 and 2.

Rows 19 and 20: With same scrap color, rep Rows 11 and 12.

Rep Rows 1–20, changing to new scrap color on each Row 11, until afghan measures approx 58 inches.

Rep Rows 1–10 once.

Top Border

Row 1 (RS): With MC, knit.

Rows 2–5: Knit.

Bind off.

Side Border

Hold afghan with right side facing you and one long edge at top. With MC, pick up and knit 220 sts evenly spaced along edge.

Row 1 (WS): Knit.

Rows 2–4: Rep Row 1.

Bind off.

Repeat on other long side.

Weave in all ends.

Design by Melissa Leapman

Skill Level

EASY

Size

About 56 inches wide x 15 inches long

Materials

- Bulky weight yarn (6 oz/108 yds/170g per ball): 6 balls pewter #152

Note: *Our photographed poncho was made with Lion Brand Wool-Ease Thick & Quick.*
- Size 13 (9mm) circular knitting needle or size needed to obtain gauge
- Stitch markers

Gauge

10 sts and 14 rows = 4 inches/10cm in stockinette st (knit one row, purl one row)

Special Abbreviation

Make 1 (M1): Inc 1 by inserting LH needle from front to back under horizontal strand between st just worked and next st, knit into the back of this loop.

Pattern Notes

Poncho is worked in one piece from neck down.

When working stockinette st on circular needles all rnds are knit.

Poncho

Cast on 56 sts.

Neck Ribbing

Rnd 1: *K1, p1; rep from * around.

Rep Rnd 1 until ribbing measures about 9 inches from cast-on edge.

Shoulders

Rnd 1: K26 for back, place marker, k2 for side seam, place marker, k26 for front, place marker, k2 for side seam, place marker.

Rnd 2: Knit to first marker, **M1** *(see Special Abbreviation)*, slip marker, k2, slip marker, M1, knit to next marker, M1, slip marker, k2, slip marker, M1. (60 sts)

Rnds 3–12: Rep Rnd 2. (100 sts)

Body

Note: *Continue to slip markers as you come to them.*

Rnd 1: Knit.

Rnd 2: [K48, M1, k2, M1] twice. (104 sts)

Rnd 3: Knit.

Rnd 4: [Knit to marker, M1, k2, M1] twice. (108 sts)

Rnds 5–8: Rep Rnds 3 and 4 twice more. (116 sts)

Rnds 9–11: Knit.

Rnd 12: [Knit to marker, M1, k2, M1] twice. (120 sts)

Rnds 13–32: [Rep Rnds 9–12] 5 times more. (140 sts)

Rnds 33–42: Knit.

Note: *When working next rnd, remove first 3 markers, leave rem marker for beg of rnd.*

Rnd 43: Purl.

Rnd 44: *K2 tog, YO, k5; rep from * around.

Rnd 45: Purl.

Bind off knitwise.

Fringe

Referring to fringe instructions on page 21 make fringe. Cut 16-inch lengths of yarn. For each knot use 6 strands. Tie knots in each YO of Rnd 44. Trim ends evenly.

Simply Snuggly

Design by Melissa Leapman

Skill Level

EASY

Sizes

Woman's small (medium, large, extra-large)

Instructions are given for smallest size, with larger sizes in parentheses. When only 1 number is given, it applies to all sizes.

Finished Measurement

Chest: 40 (41½, 45, 49) inches

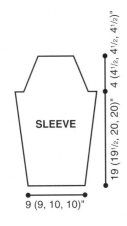

SLEEVE

4 (4½, 4½, 4½)"

19 (19½, 20, 20)"

9 (9, 10, 10)"

4 (4, 4, 4½)"

FRONT & BACK

16 (16½, 16½, 17)"

8 (8½, 9, 9)"

20 (20¾, 22½, 24½)"

Materials

- Super bulky weight yarn (6 oz/108 yds/170g per ball): 8 (9, 10, 11) balls charcoal #149

6 SUPER BULKY

Note: *Our photographed sweater was made with Lion Brand Wool-Ease Thick & Quick.*
- Size 13 (9mm) knitting needles or size needed to obtain gauge
- Size 11 (8mm) 16-inch circular knitting needle (for neckband)
- Two stitch holders
- Stitch marker

Gauge

9 sts and 20 rows = 4 inches/10cm in garter stitch (knit every row) with larger needles

To save time, take time to check gauge.

Special Abbreviation

Increase (inc): Inc 1 st by knitting in front and back of next st.

Back

With larger needles, cast on 47 (49, 53, 57) sts.

Row 1 (RS): Knit.

Row 2: Knit

Work in garter st until piece measures 16 (16½, 16½, 17) inches from cast-on edge, ending by working a WS row.

Armhole shaping

For small and medium sizes only

Row 1 (RS): Bind off 3 sts; knit across. (44, 46 sts)

Row 2: Bind off 3 sts; knit across. (41, 43 sts)

Row 3: K1, k2tog; knit to last 3 sts, k2tog-tbl; k1. (39, 41 sts)

Row 4: Knit.

Rows 5–10: Rep Rows 3 and 4 three times more. (33, 35 sts)

Work even in garter st until armholes measure 8 (8½) from cast-on edge, ending by working a WS row.

Continue with Shoulder shaping.

For large size only

Row 1 (RS): Bind off 4 sts; knit across. (49 sts)

Row 2: Bind off 4 sts; knit across. (45 sts)

Row 3: K1, k2tog, knit to last 3 sts, k2tog-tbl, k1. (43 sts)

Row 4: Rep Row 3. (41 sts)

Row 5: K1, k2tog, knit to last 3 sts, k2tog-tbl, k1.

Row 6: Knit.

Rows 7–10: [Rep Rows 5 and 6] twice more. (35 sts)

Work even in garter st until armholes measure 9 inches from cast-on edge, ending by working a WS row.

Continue with Shoulder shaping.

For extra-large size only

Row 1 (RS): Bind off 4 sts, knit across. (53 sts)

Row 2: Bind off 4 sts, knit across. (49 sts)

Row 3: K1, k2tog, knit to last 3 sts, k2tog-tbl, k1. (47 sts)

Rows 4 and 5: Rep Row 3. (43 sts)

Row 6: K1, k2tog, knit to last 3 sts, k2tog-tbl, k1.

Row 7: Knit.

Rows 8–11: [Rep Rows 6 and 7] twice more. (37 sts)

Work even in garter st until armholes measure 9 inches from cast-on edge, ending by working a WS row.

Continue with Shoulder shaping.

Shoulder shaping

For small and large sizes only

Row 1 (RS): Bind off 3 sts; knit across.

Rows 2–6: Rep Row 1. At end of Row 6, sl rem 15 (17) sts onto holder for back neck.

Continue with Front.

For medium and extra-large sizes

Row 1 (RS): Bind off 3 sts; knit across.

Rows 2–4: Rep Row 1. (23, 25 sts)

Row 5: Bind off 4 sts, knit across.

Row 6: Bind off 4 sts, sl rem 15 (17) sts onto holder for back neck.

Continue with Front.

Front

Work until number of rows and shaping are same as for Back to armhole shaping and until armhole measures 6 (6½, 7, 7), ending by working a WS row.

Neck shaping

Row 1 (RS): K13 (14, 13, 14) sts for left shoulder; sl next 7 (7, 9, 9) sts onto holder for front neck; join second skein of yarn and knit rem sts for right shoulder.

Note: *Work both sides of front at the same time using separate skeins of yarn.*

Row 2: Knit.

Row 3: For left shoulder, knit to last 3 sts, k2tog, k1; on right shoulder, k1, k2tog; knit across.

Rows 4–9: [Rep Rows 2 and 3] 3 times more. (9, 10, 9, 10 sts on each shoulder)

Row 10: Rep Row 2.

Work even in garter st until number of rows and measurement is same as Back to Shoulder shaping, ending by working a WS row.

Shoulder shaping

For small and large sizes only

Row 1 (RS): Bind off 3 sts; knit across rem sts.

Rows 2–4: Rep Row 1. (3 sts on each shoulder)

Row 5: Bind off 3 sts on left shoulder; knit across right shoulder.

Row 6: Bind off 3 rem sts.

Continue with Sleeve.

For medium and extra-large sizes only

Row 1 (RS): Bind off 3 sts; knit across rem sts.

Rows 2–4: Rep Row 1. (4 sts on each shoulder)

Row 5: Bind off 4 sts on left shoulder; knit across right shoulder.

Row 6: Bind off rem 4 sts.

Continue with Sleeve.

Sleeve

Make 2

With larger needles, cast on 22 (22, 24, 24) sts.

Row 1 (RS): Knit.

Rows 2–12: Rep Row 1.

Row 13: K1, **inc** *(see Special Abbreviation)*, knit to last 2 sts, inc, k1. (24, 24, 26, 26 sts)

Rows 14–73 (85, 85, 85): [Rep Rows 2–13] five (6, 6, 6) times more. (34, 36, 38, 38 sts)

Work even in garter st until piece measures 19 (19½, 20, 20) inches from cast-on edge, ending by working a WS row.

Cap shaping

Row 1 (RS): Bind off 3 (3, 4, 4) sts, knit across. (31, 33, 34, 34 sts)

Row 2: Bind off 3 (3, 4, 4) sts, knit across. (28, 30, 30, 30 sts)

Row 3: K1, k2tog, knit to last 3 sts; k2tog, k1. (26, 28, 28, 28 sts)

Row 4: Knit.

Rows 5–16 (18, 18, 18): [Rep Rows 3 and 4] 6 (7, 7, 7) times more. (14 sts)

Row 17 (19, 19, 19, 19): Bind off 1 st, knit across. (13 sts)

Row 18 (20, 20, 20): Bind off 1 st, knit across. (12 sts)

Rows 19 (21, 21, 21) and 20 (22, 22, 22): Rep last 2 rows. (10 sts)

Bind off all sts.

Assembly

Sew shoulder seams. Sew sleeves to body matching center of bound-off edge of sleeves to shoulder seams and easing as necessary to fit. Sew sleeve and side seams.

Neck band

Rnd 1: Hold piece with RS of back facing; with circular needle, knit 15 (15, 17, 17) sts from back neck holder, pick up and knit 10 sts evenly spaced along left front neck edge, knit 7 (7, 9, 9) sts from front neck holder, pick up and knit 10 sts along right front neck edge. (42, 42, 46, 45 sts)

Place marker at beg of rnd.

Rnd 2: *K1, p1; rep from * around.

Rep Rnd 2 until neckband measures 8 inches.

Bind off loosely in ribbing.

Colorful Stripes Turtleneck

Design by Scarlet Taylor

Skill Level

EASY

Sizes

Woman's extra-small (small, medium, large, extra-large)

Instructions are given for smallest size, with larger sizes in parentheses. When only 1 number is given, it applies to all sizes.

Finished Measurements

Chest: 33 (36, 41, 44, 49) inches

Length: 21½ (22, 22¾, 23¼, 23¼) inches

Materials

- Worsted weight yarn, (6 oz/290 yds/170g per skein): 2 (3, 3, 3, 4) skeins rose #3710 (C); 1 skein each plum #3534 (A) and celery #3625 (B)

Note: *Our photographed sweater was made with Red Heart TLC Amore.*

- Size 6 (4.25mm) 16-inch circular knitting needle (for neck band)
- Size 8 (5mm) knitting needles or size needed to obtain gauge
- Stitch marker
- Stitch holders

Gauge

18 sts and 24 rows = 4 inches/10cm in Knit 3, Purl 3 Ribbing pat with larger needles

To save time, take time to check gauge.

Special Abbreviations

Slip, Slip, Knit (ssk): Sl next 2 sts knitwise one at a time from left to right needle, insert LH needle through fronts of these sts and k2tog to dec 1 st.

Make 1 (M1): Inc 1 by inserting LH needle from front to back under horizontal strand between st just worked and next st, knit into the back of this loop.

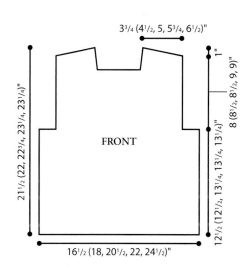

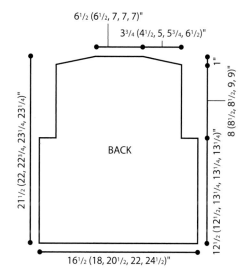

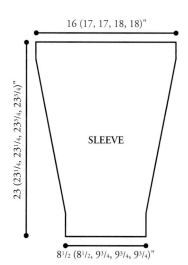

Pattern Stitches

Knit 3, Purl 3 Ribbing Pattern

Row 1 (RS): K1, *k3, p3; rep from * to last st, k1.

Row 2: P1, *k3, p3; rep from * to last st, p1.

Rep Rows 1 and 2 for pat.

Stripe Pattern

For extra-small and small sizes only

Work in Knit 3, Purl 3 Ribbing pat with 15 rows each of A, B, C, B, A.

For medium, large, and extra-large sizes only

Work in Knit 3, Purl 3 Ribbing pat with 16 rows each of A, B, C, B, end pat with 15 rows A.

Back

With larger needles and A, cast on 74 (80, 92, 98, 110) sts.

Work in Knit 3, Purl 3 Ribbing in Stripe pat, until piece measures approx 12½ (12½, 13¼, 13¼, 13¼) inches from beg, ending with a WS row (last row of Stripe pat).

Armhole shaping

With C, bind off 5 (5, 7, 7, 9) sts at beg of next 2 rows. (64, 70, 78, 84, 92 sts)

With C, continue even in Knit 3, Purl 3 Ribbing pat as established, until piece measures approx 20½ (21, 21¾, 22¼, 22¼) inches from beg, ending with a WS row.

Shoulder shaping

Row 1 (RS): Bind off 5 (6, 7, 8, 10) sts, work in pat across.

Row 2: Rep Row 1. (12, 14, 16, 18, 20 sts on each side)

Row 3: Bind off 6 (7, 8, 9, 10) sts, work in pat across.

Rows 4–6: Rep Row 3.

Sl rem 30 (30, 32, 32, 32) sts onto st holder for back neck.

Front

Work same as back until piece measures approx 18¾ (19¼, 20, 20½, 20½) inches from beg, ending with a WS row.

Neck shaping

Row 1 (RS): Work in pat as established across 26 (29, 32, 35, 39) sts; sl next 12 (12, 14, 14, 14) sts onto stitch holder; join 2nd skein of yarn, work in pat across rem 26 (29, 32, 35, 39) sts.

Note: *Work both sides at same time with separate skeins of yarn.*

Row 2: Work in pat across first side; on second side bind off 4 sts, work in pat across.

Row 3: Work in pat across first side; on second side bind off 4 sts, work in pat across. (22, 25, 28, 31, 35 sts on each side)

Row 4: Work even in pat across both sides.

Row 5: Work in pat across first side to last 3 sts, k2tog, k1; on second side, k1, **ssk** *(see Special Abbreviations),* work in pat across. (21, 24, 27, 30, 34 sts on each side)

Rows 6–13: [Rep Rows 4 and 5] 4 times more. (17, 20, 23, 26, 30 sts on each side)

Row 14: Rep Row 4.

Work even in pat, if necessary, until piece measures same as back to shoulders, ending with a WS row.

Shoulder shaping

Row 1 (RS): Bind off 5 (6, 7, 8, 10) sts, work in pat across.

Row 2: Rep Row 1. (12, 14, 16, 18, 20 sts on each side)

Row 3: Bind off 6 (7, 8, 9, 10) sts, work in pat across.

Row 4: Rep Row 3. (6, 7, 8, 9, 10 sts on each side)

Row 5: Bind off rem 6 (7, 8, 9, 10) sts on first side, work in pat across second side.

Row 6: Bind off rem 6 (7, 8, 9, 10) sts.

Sleeves

Make 2

With larger needles and C, cast on 38 (38, 44, 44, 44) sts.

Work in Knit 3, Purl 3 Ribbing pat, inc 1 st by **M1** *(see Special Abbreviations)* at each end [every 4th row] 0 (1, 0, 0, 1) time(s), [every 6th row] 13 (18, 7, 19, 18) times, then [every 8th row] 4 (0, 9, 0, 0) times. (72, 76, 76, 82, 82 sts)

Work even in pat as established until piece measures approx 23 (23¼, 23¼, 23¾, 23¾) inches from beg, ending with a WS row.

Bind off all sts.

Assembly

Sew shoulder seams.

Neck Band

With RS facing you and beg at right shoulder seam with circular needle and C, knit 30 (30, 32, 32, 32) sts from back neck holder, pick up and knit 9 (9, 7, 7, 7) sts along left front neck edge, knit 12 (12, 14, 14, 14) sts from front neck holder, pick up and knit 9 (9, 7, 7, 7) sts along right front neck edge. (60 sts)

Place marker on needle to mark beg of rnd.

Rnd 1: *K3, p3; rep from * around.

Rep Rnd 1 until neck band measures approx 5 inches.

Bind off loosely in ribbing.

Finishing

Sew sleeves to body, matching center of last row of sleeve to shoulder seam.

Sew sleeve and side seams.

Judith Ann

Design by Kathleen Power Johnson

Skill Level

EASY

Sizes

Woman's small (medium, large, extra-large, 2X-large) Instructions are given for smallest size, with larger sizes in parentheses. When only 1 number is given, it applies to all sizes.

Finished Measurements

Chest: 35 (38½, 43, 48, 51¼) inches

Length: 21 (21½, 22, 23, 24) inches

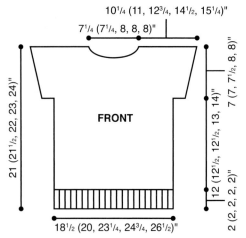

Materials

- Bulky (chunky) weight yarn (1.76 oz/68 yd/50g per ball): 5 (6, 7, 8) balls ecru #9113

Note: *Our photographed sweater was made with Moda Dea Aerie.*
- Size 15 (10mm) knitting needles or size needed to obtain gauge
- Stitch holders
- 3½ yds ⅛-inch-wide double-faced satin ribbon

Gauge

10 sts and 14 rows = 4 inches/10cm in stockinette st (knit one row, purl one row)

To save time, take time to check gauge.

Special Abbreviation

Increase (inc): Inc 1 st by knitting (or purling) in front and back of next st.

Back

Cast on 46 (50, 58, 62, 66) sts.

Ribbing

Row 1: K2, *p2, k2; rep from * across.

Row 2: P2, *k2, p2; rep from * across.

Rep Rows 1 and 2 until piece measures 2 inches.

Body

Row 1 (RS): Knit.

Row 2: Purl.

Rows 3–54 (56, 56, 58, 64): Rep Rows 1 and 2.

Row 55 (57, 57, 59, 65): Cast on 4 (4, 4, 5, 5) sts for sleeve, knit across. (59, 61, 61, 64, 70 sts)

Row 56 (58, 58, 60, 66): Cast on 4 (4, 4, 5, 5) sts for sleeve, purl across. (63, 65, 65, 69, 75 sts)

Row 57 (59, 59, 61, 67): Inc *(see Special Abbreviation)*, knit across. (64, 66, 66, 70, 76 sts)

Row 58 (60, 60, 62, 68): Inc, purl across. (65, 67, 67, 71, 77 sts)

[Rep last 2 rows] 7 (7, 9, 10, 7) times more. (70, 74, 84, 92, 96 sts)

[Rep Rows 1 and 2] 7 (7, 6, 6, 9) times.

Next Row: Bind off 26 (28, 32, 36, 38) sts; knit next 18 (18, 20, 20, 20) sts and place on stitch holder; bind off rem 26 (28, 32, 36, 38) sts.

Front

Work same as Back until there are 70 (74, 84, 92, 96) sts on needle, ending with a WS row.

Neck & Shoulder shaping

Row 1 (RS): For left shoulder, knit 30 (32, 36, 40, 42); join second ball of yarn, for neck, knit 10 (10, 12, 12, 12) sts and place on st holder; for right shoulder, knit rem sts. (30, 32, 36, 40, 42 sts on each shoulder)

Note: *Work both shoulders at same time with separate balls of yarn.*

Row 2: For right shoulder, purl across; for left shoulder, bind off 2 sts, purl across.

Row 3: For left shoulder, knit across, for right shoulder, bind off 2 sts. (28, 30, 34, 38, 40 sts on each shoulder)

Rows 4 and 5: Rep Rows 2 and 3. (26, 28, 32, 36, 38 sts on each shoulder)

Row 6: Purl across both shoulders.

Row 7: Knit across both shoulders.

Row 8: Purl across both shoulders.

Bind off all sts.

Assembly

Sew right shoulder seam.

Edgings

Neck Edging

With RS facing, beginning at left front shoulder, pick up and knit 5 sts along left front neck edge, knit 10 (10, 12, 12, 12) sts from front neck holder, 5 sts along right neckline, knit 18 (18,

20, 20, 20) sts from back neck stitch holder. (38, 38, 42, 42, 42 sts)

Bind off as to knit.

Sew left shoulder seam.

Sleeve Edging

With RS facing, beg in row after cast on sts, pick up and knit 34 (34, 36, 39, 39) sts evenly around armhole, ending at last row before second set of cast on sts.

Bind off as to knit.

Finishing

Sew side seams, including sts cast on for sleeves.

Thread 1½ yds of ribbon into tapestry needle. Insert needle to left of center front neckline and pull through, leaving a 10-inch tail. Loosely overcast around neck edging to center front. Tie in bow and trim ends.

Thread 1 yd of ribbon into tapestry needle and insert at one underarm seam. Loosely overcast around each sleeve edge and fasten off.

Repeat for other sleeve edge.

Casual Rugby Pullover

Design by Melissa Leapman

Skill Level

EASY

Sizes

Woman's small (medium, large, extra-large) Instructions are given for smallest size, with larger sizes in parentheses. When only 1 number is given, it applies to all sizes.

Finished Measurements

Chest: 34 (36, 40, 43) inches

Length: 22½ (23, 23½, 24) inches

Materials

- Bulky weight yarn (6 oz/185 yds/170g per skein): 3 (4, 4, 5) skeins Corinthian #345 (A), 1 skein each (for all sizes) sunshine state #372 (B) and coral gables #370 (C)

5 BULKY

Note: *Our photographed sweater was made with Lion Brand Homespun.*
- Size 9 (5.5mm) straight and 16-inch circular (for neck band) knitting needles
- Size 10 (6mm) knitting needles or size needed to obtain gauge
- Stitch markers
- Stitch holders

Gauge

12 sts = 4 inches/10cm in St st (knit one row, purl one row) with larger needles

To save time, take time to check gauge.

Special Abbreviations

Slip, Slip, Knit (ssk): Slip next 2 sts, one at a time as to knit from left needle to right needle. Insert left needle in front of both sts and k2 tog to decrease 1 st.

Increase (inc) Inc 1 st by knitting in front and back of next st.

Stripe Pattern

Row 1: With B, knit.
Row 2: With B, purl.
Rows 3 and 4: Rep Rows 1 and 2.
Row 5: With A, knit.
Row 6: With A, purl.
Row 7: With C, knit.
Row 8: With C, purl.
Rows 9–14: [Rep Rows 7 and 8] 3 times.
Rows 15 and 16: Rep Rows 5 and 6.
Rows 17–20: [Rep Rows 1 and 2] twice.

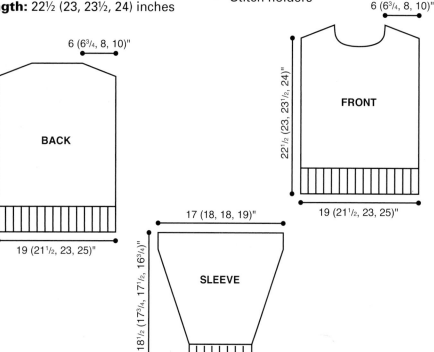

Back

Ribbing

With smaller needles and B, cast on 57 (65, 69, 75) sts. Cut B.

Row 1 (RS): With A, k1, *p1, k1; rep from * across.

Row 2: P1, *k1, p1; rep from * across.

Rep Rows 1 and 2 until ribbing measures approx 2½ inches from cast-on edge, ending by working a WS row.

Change to larger needles.

Body

Row 1 (RS): Knit.

Row 2: Purl.

Rep Rows 1 and 2 until piece measures 22 (23, 23 ½, 24) inches from cast-on edge, ending by working a WS row.

Shoulder shaping

Row 1 (RS): Bind off 6 (7, 8, 9) sts, knit across.

Row 2: Bind off 6 (7, 8, 9) sts, purl across. (45, 51, 53, 57 sts)

Rows 3 and 4: Rep Rows 1 and 2. (33, 37, 37, 39 sts)

Row 5: Bind off 6 (8, 8, 9) sts, knit across.

Row 6: Bind off 6 (8, 8, 9) sts, purl across.

Place rem 21 sts on stitch holder for back neck.

Front

Work same as for Back until piece measures approx 12 (13, 14, 15) inches from cast-on edge, ending by working a WS row.

Work Rows 1–20 of Stripe Pattern.

With A, work in St st until piece measures approx 19½ (20½, 21, 21½) inches from cast-on edge, ending by working a WS row.

Neck shaping

Row 1 (RS): K23 (27, 29, 32) for left shoulder; join second skein of yarn; k11 sts and place on holder for neck; k23 (27, 29, 32) sts for right shoulder.

Note: *Work both shoulders at same time with separate skeins of yarn.*

Row 2: Purl.

Row 3: For left shoulder, knit across; for right shoulder, bind off 2 sts, knit rem sts.

Row 4: For right shoulder, purl across; for left shoulder, bind off 2 sts, purl rem sts. (21, 25, 27, 30 sts on each shoulder)

Rows 5 and 6: Rep Rows 3 and 4. (19, 23, 25, 28 sts on each shoulder)

Row 7: For left shoulder, k16 (20, 22, 25), k2tog, k1; for right shoulder, k1, **ssk** *(see Special Abbreviation)*, knit rem sts. (18, 22, 24, 27 sts on each shoulder)

Row 8: Purl.

Row 9: Knit.

Row 10: Purl.

Shoulder shaping

Row 1 (RS): Bind off 6 (7, 8, 9) sts, knit across.

Row 2: Bind off 6 (7, 8, 9) sts, purl across. (12, 15, 16, 18 sts on each shoulder)

Rows 3 and 4: Rep Rows 1 and 2. (6, 8, 8, 9 sts on each shoulder)

Row 5: For left shoulder, bind off rem 6 (8, 8, 9) sts; on right shoulder, knit across.

Row 6: For right shoulder, bind off rem sts.

Sleeve

Make 2

Note: *If using a yarn color that is self-striping, it is necessary to start at the same place in the color sequence on each sleeve for the sleeves to match.*

Ribbing

With smaller needles and B, cast on 27 (27, 29, 29) sts. Cut B.

Row 1 (RS): With A, k1, *p1, k1; rep from * across.

Row 2: P1, *k1, p1, rep from * across.

Rep Rows 1 and 2 until piece measures approx 2½ inches from cast-on edge, ending with a WS row.

Change to larger needles.

Body

Row 1 (RS): Inc *(see Special Abbreviations)*, knit to next to last 2 sts, inc, k1. (29, 29, 31, 31 sts)

Row 2: Purl.

Row 3: Knit.

Row 4: Purl.

Rows 5–16 (44, 36, 56): [Rep Rows 1–4] 3 (10, 8, 12) times more. (35, 49, 47, 55 sts)

Next 2 rows: Rep Rows 3 and 4.

For small, medium and large size only

Continue in St st, inc one st each end of next row and every 6th row until there are 51 (55, 55) sts on needle.

Continue with For All Sizes.

For extra-large size only

Continue with For All Sizes.

For All Sizes

Work in St st until sleeve measures approx 18½ (17¾, 17½, 16¾) inches from cast-on edge, ending by working a WS row.

Bind off.

Assembly

Sew shoulder seams.

Neck Ribbing

Hold sweater with right shoulder and RS facing, with circular needle and A, pick up and knit 21 sts from back neck holder, pick up and knit 9 (10, 10, 11) sts evenly spaced along left front neck edge, knit 11 sts from front neck holder, pick up and knit 9 (10, 10, 11) sts evenly spaced along left neck edge. (50, 52, 52, 54 sts)

Rnd 1: *K1, p1; rep from * around.

Rep Rnd 1 until ribbing measures 1 inch. Change to B.

Bind off loosely in ribbing.

Finishing

Mark 8½ (9, 9, 9½) inches from shoulder seam on front and back. Sew sleeves to body between markers matching center of last row of sleeves to shoulder seams. Sew sleeve and side seams.

Blue Ridge Mountains Pullover

Design by George Shaheen

Skill Level

EASY

Size

Woman's size small (medium, large, extra-large)

Instructions are given for smallest size, with larger sizes in parentheses. When only 1 number is given, it applies to all sizes.

Finished Measurement

Chest: 38 (42, 46, 50) inches

Materials

- Bulky weight yarn (3 oz/135 yds/85g per ball): 6 (7, 8, 9) balls heather blue #111(MC); 2 (2, 2, 3) balls plum #145 (CC)

5 BULKY

Note: *Our photographed pullover was made with Lion Brand Jiffy.*

- Size 10.5 (6.5mm) 16-inch circular and straight knitting needles, or size required for gauge
- Size 11 (8mm) 16-inch circular and straight knitting needles
- Tapestry needle
- Stitch holder

Gauge

19 sts and 36 rows = 6 inches in pattern stitch with smaller needles

To save time, take time to check gauge.

Special Abbreviations

With yarn in front (wyif): Hold yarn in front of work while slipping the indicated number of sts. ***Note:*** *It may be necessary to move yarn under needle to back of work after slipping sts.*

Slip (sl): Slip st from left needle to right needle inserting right needle as if to purl, unless otherwise stated.

BACK

21 (21, 21, 21)"

19 (21, 23, 25)"

$8^{1/2}$ ($8^{1/2}$, $8^{3/4}$, $8^{3/4}$)"

$12^{1/2}$ ($12^{1/2}$, $12^{1/4}$, $12^{1/4}$)"

6 ($6^{1/2}$, 7, $7^{1/2}$)"

$6^{1/2}$ ($7^{1/4}$, 8, $8^{3/4}$)"

6 ($6^{3/4}$, 7, 7)"

$8^{1/2}$ ($8^{1/2}$, $8^{3/4}$, $8^{3/4}$)"

21 (21, 21)"

FRONT

$12^{1/2}$ ($12^{1/2}$, $12^{1/4}$, $12^{1/4}$)"

19 (21, 23, 25)"

SLEEVE

18 (18, 18, 18)"

$16^{3/4}$ ($16^{3/4}$, $17^{1/2}$, $17^{1/2}$)"

Back

With MC and smaller straight needles, cast on 61 (67, 72, 79) sts.

Row 1 (RS): Knit.

Row 2: K5 (3, 3, 4), **sl** 1 *(see Special Abbreviations)*, **wyif** *(see Special Abbreviations)*; *****k4, sl 1 wyif; rep from ***** 9 (11, 12, 13) times more; k5 (3, 3, 4).

Rows 3–126: Rep Rows 1 and 2.

Row 127: Bind off 21 (23, 25, 28) sts; knit until there are 19 (21, 22, 23) sts on right needle; bind off rem 21 (23, 25, 28) sts.

Place sts on holder for back neck.

Mark 8½ (8½, 8¾, 8¾) inches down from bind off on each side for armhole.

Front

With MC and smaller straight needles, cast on 61 (67, 72, 79) sts.

Row 1 (RS): Knit.

Row 2: K5 (3, 3, 4), sl 1; *****k4, sl 1; rep from ***** 9 (11, 12, 13) times more; k5 (3, 3, 4).

Rows 3–90 (86, 84, 84): [Rep Rows 1 and 2] 44 (42, 41, 41) times more.

Neck shaping

Row 1 (RS): For left shoulder, k21 (23, 25, 28) sts; join second ball of MC, for neck, bind off 19 (21, 22, 23) sts; for right shoulder, knit rem sts.

Note: *Work both shoulders at same time with separate balls of yarn.*

Row 2: For right shoulder, k5 (1, 2, 1), sl 1, [k4, sl 1] 2 (4, 4, 5) times, k5 (1, 2, 1); for left shoulder k5 (1, 2, 1), sl 1, [k4, sl 1] 2 (4, 4, 5) times, k5 (1, 2, 1).

Row 3: Knit across both shoulders.

Rows 4–23 (27, 29, 29): [Rep Rows 2 and 3] 10 (12, 13, 13) times more.

Row 24 (28, 30, 30): Rep Row 2. Fasten off MC.

Row 25 (29, 31, 31): Attach CC and knit across left shoulder; join second ball of CC and knit across right shoulder.

Rows 26 (30, 32, 32)–36 (40, 42, 42): Knit across both shoulders.

Row 37 (41, 43, 43): Bind off both shoulders.

Mark 8½ (8½, 8¾, 8¾) inches down from bind off on each side for armhole.

Sleeves

Make 2
Cuff

With CC and larger straight needles, cast on 53 (53, 55, 55) sts.

Knit every row until cuff measures 2½ inches.

Change to MC and smaller straight needles.

Note: *When not in use, carry blue loosely up side edge. Cut and attach CC as needed.*

Body

Row 1 (RS): With MC, knit.

Row 2: K1 (1, 2, 2), sl 1; *****k4, sl 1; rep from ***** 9 times more; k1 (1, 2, 2).

Rows 3–10: [Rep Row 1 and 2] 4 times more. At end of Row 10, drop MC.

Row 11: With CC, knit.

Row 12: Knit. At end of row, fasten off CC.

Rows 13–108: [Rep Rows 1–12] 8 times more.

At end of Row 108, bind off. Weave in all ends.

Finishing

Block pieces to measurements.

Sew shoulder seams.

Collar

Hold with RS front facing and cast-on edge to right. Beg in right corner of neck edge with smaller circular needle and CC, pick up and knit 19 (21, 22, 22) sts along right neck edge; knit 19 (21, 22, 23) sts from back neck stitch holder; pick up and knit 19 (21, 22, 22) sts along left neck edge. (57, 63, 66, 67 sts)

Knit every row until collar measures 1½ inches from beg.

Change to larger circular needle and knit every row until collar measures 3¾ (4, 4¼, 4½) inches from beg, ending with a RS row.

Bind off.

Assembly

Pin edges of collar along front neck edge, with bound-off edges meeting at center front. Sew in place, easing as necessary to fit. Sew sleeves to body between markers, matching center of sleeves to shoulder seams. Sew sleeve seams, reversing seam at cuff. Sew side seams, leaving 5 inches open at bottom for side slit.

Baby Footies

Design by Kathy Wesley

Skill Level

EASY

Finished Measurements

Cuff: Approx 3½ inches

Foot: Approx 4 inches from heel to toe

Materials

- Sock weight yarn (203 yds/50g per ball): *for variegated cuff version:* 1 ball hippi hot #40743 (A), 1 ball lime hot #40712 (B); *for two-tone cuff version:* 1 ball aqua hot #40742 (C), 1 ball icy hot #40005 (D)

1 SUPER FINE

Note: *Our photographed projects were completed with Sox from Bernat.*

- Size 4 (3.5mm) needles or size needed to obtain gauge
- Size 7 (4.5mm) needles
- Stitch holders

Gauge

14 sts = 2 inches/5cm in garter st

To save time, take time to check gauge.

Variegated Cuff

With B and larger needles, cast on 42 sts.

Row 1 (RS): K2, [p3, k2] 8 times.

Row 2: P2, [k3, p2] 8 times.

Rows 3–6: [Rep Rows 1 and 2] twice. Cut B.

Row 7: With A, knit.

Row 8: P2, [k3, p2] 8 times.

Rows 9–24: [Rep Rows 1 and 2] 8 times.

Change to smaller needles and continue with ribbing.

Two-Tone Cuff

With C and larger needles, cast on 42 sts.

Row 1 (RS): K2, [p3, k2] 8 times.

Row 2: P2, [k3, p2] 8 times.

Rows 3–6: [Rep Rows 1 and 2] twice. Cut C.

Row 7: With D, knit.

Row 8: P2, [k3, p2] 8 times.

Rows 9–12: [Rep Rows 1 and 2] twice. Cut D.

Row 13: With C, knit.

Row 14: Rep Row 8.

Rows 15–18: [Rep Rows 1 and 2] twice. Cut C.

Row 19: With D, knit.

Row 20: Rep Row 8.

Rows 21–24: [Rep Rows 1 and 2] twice. Cut D.

Change to smaller needles and C, continue with ribbing.

Ribbing

Row 1 (RS): [P1, k1] 4 times, p1, *k2 tog, [p1, k1] 4 times, p1; rep from * twice more. (39 sts)

Row 2: K1, *p1, k1; rep from * across.

Row 3: P1, *k1, p1; rep from * across.

Row 4: Rep Row 2.

Instep

Row 1 (RS): P1, [k1, p1] 13 times, sl rem 12 sts onto stitch holder.

Row 2: K1, [p1, k1] 7 times, sl rem 12 sts onto 2nd stitch holder.

Row 3: P1, [k1, p1] 7 times.

Row 4: K1, [p1, k1] 7 times.

Rep Rows 3 and 4 until instep measures 1¾ inches, ending with a Row 4.

Cut yarn, leaving sts on needle.

Foot

With RS facing and instep to left, knit across 12 sts on first holder, pick up and knit 14 sts along side edge of instep, knit across 15 instep sts, pick up and knit 14 sts along other side of instep, knit 12 sts from 2nd holder. (67 sts)

Rows 1–11: Knit.

Sole

Row 1 (RS): K4, k2 tog, k20, k2 tog, k11, k2 tog, k20, k2 tog, k4. (63 sts)

Row 2 and all even-numbered rows: Knit.

Row 3: K3, k2 tog, k20, k2 tog, k9, k2 tog, k20, k2 tog, k3. (59 sts)

Row 5: K2, k2 tog, k20, k2 tog, k7, k2 tog, k20, k2 tog, k2. (55 sts)

Row 7: K1, k2 tog, k20, k2 tog, k5, k2 tog, k20, k2 tog, k1. (52 sts)

Row 9: K2 tog, knit to last 2 sts, k2 tog. (49 sts)

Bind off knitwise. Fasten off yarn, leaving an 8-inch end for sewing.

Finishing

With tapestry needle, sew bottom and back seam.

Basket Weave Baby Sweater

Design by Edie Eckman

Skill Level

EASY

Sizes

Newborn to 6 months (9 to 12, 18 to 24) months

Finished Measurements

Finished Chest: 19 (22, 25) inches

Finished Length: 10½ (12, 14½) inches

Materials

- D.K. weight yarn (5 oz/459 yds/140g per ball): 1 (1, 2) balls spring green #176

Note: Our photographed sweater was made with Lion Brand Babysoft.

- Size 6 (4mm) needles or size needed to obtain gauge
- 4 (⅝-inch-diameter) buttons

Gauge

5 sts and 8 rows = 4 inches/10cm in Basket Weave pat

To save time, take time to check gauge.

Special Abbreviation

Increase (inc): Inc 1 st by knitting in the front and back of stitch.

Pattern Stitch

Basket Weave Pattern

Multiple of 8 sts

Rows 1 (WS): K3, *p2, k6; rep from * to last 5 sts, p2, k3.

Row 2: P3, *k2, p6; rep from * to last 5 sts, k2, p3.

Row 3: K3, *p2, k6; rep from * to last 5 sts, p2, k3.

Row 4: Knit.

Row 5: K7, *p2, k6; rep from * to last st, k1.

Row 6: P7, *k2, p6; rep from * to last st, p1.

Row 7: K7, *p2, k6; rep from * to last st, k1.

Row 8: Knit.

Rep Rows 1–8 for pat.

Back

Ribbing

Cast on 48 (56, 64) sts.

Row 1 (WS): P3, *k2, p2; rep from * to last st, p1.

Row 2: K3, *p2, k2; rep from * to last st, k1.

Rows 3–6: [Rep Rows 1 and 2] twice more.

Row 7: P3, *k2, p2; rep from * to last st, p1.

Row 8: Knit.

Body

Work Rows 1–8 of Basket Weave pat until piece measures 9½ (11½, 13½) inches from cast-on edge, ending with a Row 4 or Row 8.

Neck and Shoulder ribbing

Row 1 (WS): P3, *k2, p2; rep from * to last st, p1.

Row 2: K3, *p2, k2; rep from * to last st, k1.

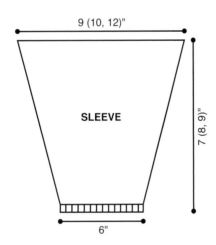

9 (10, 12)"

SLEEVE

7 (8, 9)"

6"

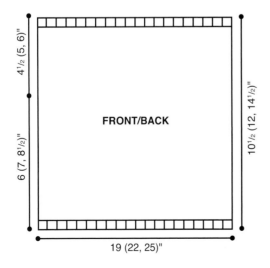

4½ (5, 6)"

FRONT/BACK

6 (7, 8½)"

10½ (12, 14½)"

19 (22, 25)"

Rows 3–8: [Rep Rows 1 and 2] 3 times more.

Bind off knitwise on WS.

Front

Work same as Back to Neck and Shoulder ribbing.

Neck and Shoulder ribbing

Row 1 (WS): P3, *k2, p2; rep from * to last st, p1.

Row 2: K3, *p2, k2; rep from * to last st, k1.

Row 3: P3, *k2, p2; rep from * to last st, p1.

Row 4: P3, k2, p2 (k2, yo, p2tog) twice, (k2, p2) 4 (6, 8) times, (k2, p2tog, yo) twice, k2, p2, k2, p3.

Rows 5–8: [Rep Rows 1 and 2] twice.

Bind off knitwise on WS.

Sleeves

Ribbing

Cast on 32 sts.

Row 1 (WS): P3, *k2, p2; rep from * to last st, p1.

Row 2: K3, *p2, k2; rep from * to last st, k1.

Rows 3–6: [Rep Rows 1 and 2] twice more.

Row 7: P3, *k2, p2; rep from * to last st, p1.

Row 8: Knit.

Body

Work Rows 1–8 of Basket Weave Stitch and *at the same time* **inc** *(see Special Abbreviation)* at each end of every 4th row 0 (1, 12) times then every 6th row 7 (8, 2) times, working inc sts into pat. (46, 50, 60 sts)

Work even in pat until sleeve measures 7 (8, 9) inches from cast-on edge.

Bind off all sts.

Finishing

Sew buttons to back shoulders opposite buttonholes on front. Overlap front shoulder ribbing over back shoulder ribbing and pin at armhole edge. Measure 4½ (5, 6) inches from shoulder and mark for armhole. Center last row of sleeves at shoulders and sew to body between markers. Sew side and underarm seams.

American School of Needlework ®
excellence in instruction

DRG Publishing
306 East Parr Road
Berne, IN 46711

©2005 American School of Needlework

TOLL-FREE ORDER LINE or to request a free catalog (800) 582-6643

Customer Service (800) 282-6643, **Fax** (800) 882-6643

Visit AnniesAttic.com.

ISBN:1-59012-145-7   All rights reserved.   Printed in USA   2 3 4 5 6 7 8 9